# HOW TO RAISE A MILLIONAIRE

"This book shows you how to give your child a running start at financial success in life. These wonderful ideas can change your child's life–for the rest of his/her life."

—**Brian Tracy**
Author of *The Way to Wealth*

"This kind of real world advice will help you set your kid up to succeed in life no matter what the economy looks like. Ann's simple approach is brilliant. Finally, we can start changing our kid's conversation with money and success."

—**Loral Langemeier**
Author of *The Millionaire Maker*

# HOW TO RAISE A MILLIONAIRE

*Six Millionaire Skills Parents Can Teach Their Kids
So They Can Imagine And Live The Life Of Their Dreams!*

## ANN MORGAN JAMES, Jack's Mom

*Illustrated by* Kevin Coffey

New York

# HOW TO RAISE A MILLIONAIRE

*Six Millionaire Skills Parents Can Teach Their Kids*
*So They Can Imagine And Live The Life Of Their Dreams!*

ISBN 978-1-61448-246-8 paperback
ISBN 978-1-61448-247-5 eBook
Library of Congress Control Number: 2012932230

Morgan James Publishing
The Entrepreneurial Publisher
5 Penn Plaza, 23rd Floor,
New York City, New York 10001
(212) 655-5470 office • (516) 908-4496 fax
www.MorganJamesPublishing.com

**Illustrations by:**
Kevin Coffey

**Cover Design by:**
Rachel Lopez
www.r2cdesign.com

**Interior Design by:**
Bonnie Bushman
bonnie@caboodlegraphics.com

In an effort to support local communities, raise awareness and funds, Morgan James Publishing donates a percentage of all book sales for the life of each book to Habitat for Humanity Peninsula and Greater Williamsburg.

Get involved today, visit
www.MorganJamesBuilds.com.

# DEDICATION

To my dear son, Jack: You are my inspiration. Thank you for your unquenchable spirit, which drove me to invent wacky ways to fuel your creative fire. I apologize in advance for all the money you will have to spend in therapy!

To Alex Carroll: You were a stranger who literally saw an ember burning in me and blew oxygen on it. When others, who were much closer, were trying to use a fire hose to put it out, you were my arsonist! Thank you for believing in me. You probably will never know how much that 15 minutes of your time has meant in my life. When I have self-doubt, I transport myself back to April in Manhattan when you helped me see I was not crazy, and it recharges me again. Thanks! I will be forever paying it forward.

# TABLE OF CONTENTS

At the end of the Preface, the Introduction and most of the Chapters I have added external resources to help you and your munchkin in your journey to Kid Entrepreneur.

Some of these are resources I personally found helpful while others offer a different approach. The truth is; I have many cookbooks in my kitchen. I don't use all the recipes in each book, but each chef offers me a variety of options. I like options. I thought you might too.

So, at the end of each of these areas in the book, you'll find a URL to a page on our website designed just for you, my readers. I hope you find the information there helpful!

# FOREWORD

I grew up hearing, "You have to work hard for money." I was born and raised on a farm in Nebraska and I worked hard, just like my parents taught me. At 17, I started my first business and worked intensely to earn a sports scholarship to college. My upbringing served me well, but the key to successfully running and building a business is not just about working hard; it is also about working smart.

*How to Raise a Millionaire* is the first book I have seen that teaches parents how to teach their kids how to work smart at building a business. Ann's book teaches anyone, entrepreneur or not, how to help their kid start a business. She takes the process of starting a business and breaks it down into simple to follow steps. She has created a system so any child can learn but she does not stop there. Her blueprint for success is her six millionaire skills. This is the punch behind her powerful book. These skills are something every kid should know. It should be taught in our schools, but it isn't. As our global economy shifts and changes, we must give our kids an entrepreneurial mindset to succeed. An industrial mindset is no longer viable today.

This kind of real world advice will help you set your kids up to succeed in life no matter what the economy looks like. Ann's simple approach is brilliant. Finally, we can start changing our kids' conversations with money and success.

**—Loral Langemeier**
Author of *The Millionaire Maker*

# PREFACE

While this book will probably most often be read by parents, there are others who deserve a special introduction:

To all you grandparents, aunts, uncles, brothers, sisters, stepparents, family friends, and others out there taking the lead in the lives of a child, I salute you!

You are beyond special and you should know this: what you are doing is selfless and rare. We (our society) owe you a debt of gratitude.

As you read this book and see the words "your kid," I am speaking to you! You have earned the right to use the phrase with the child whom you are helping because—in fact—you are acting as their parent.

In Cub Scouts, we use the term "Akela," a character in Rudyard Kipling's *The Jungle Book*. Akela the wolf finds the lost child Mowgli and brings him up as if he were his own cub. In Cub Scouts, we refer to all adults as Akela because you never know who might be accompanying a child. It is a form of respect, and so I use it here for you.

Thank you, Akela, for the love and guidance you are giving to the child in your life. Thank you for giving them the start they otherwise would not have gotten. Thank you for making the extra effort. You are—without a doubt—my hero!

> Sometimes parents are left to care for their children's children and frankly they have little to no legal standing. This is certainly not the case with everyone. However, if you find yourself in this gut–wrenching situation, you want to play an important role in your grandchildren's lives and don't know where to turn, I hope this resource helps you.
>
> **www.howtoraiseamillionaire.com/caregiver**

# ACKNOWLEDGMENT

Saying thank you to the people who have supported Jack and me seems hardly enough. We have been blessed to have family, friends and faith to lean on and are so very grateful for the unflagging support.

The past year and a half has been exhilarating, challenging, heart wrenching, and thrilling all at the same time. Making the decision to reinvent myself at age 50 and become a writer has been a leap of faith and an adventure. One I could never have undertaken without an amazing posse.

First I would like to thank my immediate family. My brother Buck—whom I adore and admire—and Kim, my brother's devoted girlfriend of 14 years. These two amazing people are always there for me. As I was writing this, I was struggling with what to call Kim. She has been so much more than my brother's girlfriend. She has been a friend, a sister and a cheerleader all rolled into one and is very special to me. She has been more than a girlfriend to my brother. She has truly created a *home* for my brother and his family. We are all privileged to have you in our lives Kim.

I have been blessed to have my nephew Michael, my niece Michele, her boyfriend Daniel, their adorable boy Colton, Daniel's two boys Romeo and Daniel, Kim's son Joe, his wife Stacey and their daughter Kailey in my corner.

Being one of two kids has meant my immediate family is small. I have been so fortunate to have an extended family who has always felt *immediate* to me. My cousins Bob and Ellen, who are more like brother and sister to me, along with their families, Alma, Melissa, Ashley, Megan and John always give us a safe place to land. The times we spend together are special.

My cousins on my father's side are no less remarkable. Over the past year I have come to be very close with my cousin Annette and her family. Jack and I have spent some amazing moments with Annette, her husband Jerry and their three kids Jordan, Ashley and Joel. Like the rest of my family, they believe in us and give us strength. Her sisters Linda and Donna and their families are a

xviii | HOWtoRAISEaMILLIONAIRE

godsend. Uncle John and Daddy are *hangin' in heaven* smiling at the four of us girls! Jerry calls them Statler and Waldorf: the lovable curmudgeon Muppet characters who heckle the rest of the cast from their balcony seats. He is so spot on; I can hear them now laughing at their own jokes and poking fun. My dear Auntie Lois showed me what it means to be a woman of faith. There have been many times in the past year and a half when I have been very grateful for the gift she gave me.

Aristotle said, "What is a friend? A single soul dwelling in two bodies."

I have been fortunate to have friends who are beyond compare. My dear friend Melin, her husband Terry and daughter Tera have shown Jack and me love and friendship that is unequaled.

My friend Chuck, who is like a second brother, has listened to me with his heart and soul. I can't tell you how much your friendship means to me.

Our Noble family of friends—especially Sheri and Julie—are still the very best.

Our friends Bruce, Lois and Bill make our mountain lives rich. Your friendship and support are as refreshing as the air in our beloved Cassel!

I don't know what Jack and I would do without our Oakland Athletics family; you have been so supportive over this challenging and rewarding time. We love going to the games and we miss you madly in the off season. Section 219: The Unofficial Backseat Drivers of the Oakland Athletics; we love you! Go A's.

When Jack was in first grade, we went to a scout recruiting night for Pack 166. Jack immediately wanted to join the pack and become a Cub Scout; I signed up to be a den leader. I could never have known the impact that decision would have on my life. My Den 2 boys—Alec, Andy, Brian, Jeremy, Jordan, Randy and Sean—and their families are so very special to me. Each of you is extraordinary. We spent five years exploring and growing together; you have all taught me so much!

Over those five years in Pack 166, I worked with a number of fabulous parents who gave their time and talents to our pack; thank you for all you have done and continue to do for our kids.

My extended scouting family continually shows me how to *Give It*. Thank you for giving me an outlet for Jack to grow and mature into an amazing young man. So many of you give so much to the youth of our community; I only hope I can walk in your shadow.

The friendships mentioned above have been some of my longest standing friendships, but this journey has brought a number of new friends into my life and I would be remiss if I didn't mention them. God puts people in our lives we need; Mary, Sandra and Rachel have certainly been three of those people. My ability to be honest and open with you has been invaluable. I love how our lives have grown together and continue to intertwine. My LBT76 friends and my mastermind groups continue to provide great support.

In learning this new industry, I have had the pleasure of meeting so many wonderful people. Loral, James, Jonathan, Mr. Tracy, Alex, Craig and Audrey are just a few of the experts who have opened their arsenals to me. The resources you provided me have allowed me to drink in your expertise. Thank you.

I would like to take this opportunity to say a word about one of the most gracious gentlemen I have ever had the pleasure of meeting; Mr. Brian Tracy. He was holding a seminar on Personal Achievement and I thought Jack would benefit from what he had to say. It was at Mr. Tracy's seminar where Jack wrote his life's mission: to cure cancer. I have no doubt my son will achieve this lofty goal. It was not just what Mr. Tracy taught us those three days which touched Jack, but it was how he taught us. He is the master. The last morning of the session we were getting breakfast and Mr. Tracy and his lovely wife Barbara walked into the restaurant. Unbeknownst to me, Jack walked right up and asked Mr. Tracy if he would write the foreword for his book. They spoke for a few moments and Mr. Tracy graciously said, "Yes, I will write the foreword for your book." Not only was my 12 year old going to cure cancer and be a published author but now Brian Tracy was writing the foreword. Wow. Thank you, Mr. Tracy for showing Jack the gracious mark of a true gentleman. The generosity you showed Jack by taking the time to write his foreword has touched us both deeply.

Thank you to Kevin Coffey, my amazing illustrator. You have been able to bring this story to life. You are a remarkable talent.

I would like to publicly thank the management team and staff at Morgan James—in particular Scott Frishman. Your willingness to take a chance on this first-time author is humbling. I intend to do you proud.

Last I want to thank my parents. Their guidance and unconditional love taught me so many amazing lessons. I miss them both every day of my life. Until we meet again...I have so much to tell you.

This acknowledgment would not be complete if I didn't recognize my ex-husband John. Thank you John for giving me the most incredible gift anyone could ever give me: Jack.

# INTRODUCTION

## *Our Own Backyard*

Most parents want their kids to be successful. This desire has driven our society to take competition to a fever pitch to find the best schools, teachers, sports teams, ballet, gymnastics, art, and music. Parents are pushing their kids to be the best at *everything,* and have explored, exploited, and exaggerated every extracurricular activity on the planet!

In our haste to set our kids up for a wonderful life, we have forgotten to look in our own backyard—inside the four walls of our own homes. We send our kids to every expert under the sun, but then forget *we* are the "keepers of the secrets"—the secret skills to help any kid become a success at anything they desire in life.

## *Our Changing Economy*

Our world and economy have changed. In the media, we hear about it ad nauseum but they are right: it is affecting our kids. Our society has taken competitiveness to a new level. Gone are the days when you went to college, received a degree, and then got a job. It is getting more and more competitive for kids to get into the college of their choice, and admissions evaluators are looking deeper than grades when they evaluate our little darlings. When I was applying to universities, my meager 3.2 grade point average (GPA) was good enough to get me into the universities to which I applied; now, a 4.0 GPA is very likely not enough to get you past the first cut.

Kids need to hedge their bets. They must show the admissions people they are serious and dedicated. Being a business owner is a great way for our kids to set themselves apart. When they finish college, our children will find the race has just begun. College admissions departments are not the only places where change has occurred in our economy. The U.S. Bureau of Labor Statistics reported the following:

> The median number of years that wage and salary workers had been with their current employer was 4.4[1].

If we think our kids are going to work for one company, get their retirement and 401Ks funded by said company and retire at age 65 to live out their golden years in comfort and security, we are dreaming. More and more, the burden is falling on individuals to feather their own nests. It is our job as parents to help educate our kids so they are able to plan for their own retirement. I don't know about you, but when my son is 30, I'll be 70.

JACK AT 30     MOM AT 70

The last thing I want is him coming back home to Mama, plopping down on my couch and taking root. Sure, I am a good parent and if he falls short I'll be there to help out. That said: I have got to tell you, I want to do as much as I can to give him the tools he needs to succeed in any economy so he is *not* living with me in my golden years! I am working to teach Jack millionaire skills and foster in him a mindset; they are the tools he will use to succeed!

---

1    U.S. Department of Labor, Bureau of Labor Statistics, *Employee Tenure Summary*, (Washington DC, U.S. Department of Labor, September 2010)

As you can see by the table—which shows world populations and the percentage of millionaires—less than 2% of the world's population has a net worth of more than $1 million. The United States and Switzerland have the highest percentage of millionaires, coming in at a whopping 3%. The percentages for other countries drop off from there:

### High Net Worth Individuals (more than US $1 million)

| Rank | Country | Number | Population | Percent of population |
|---|---|---|---|---|
| | World | 10,000,000 | 6,809,972,000 | 0.15% |
| 1 | United States | 2,886,200 | 305,529,237 | 3.27% |
| 2 | Japan | 1,650,000 | 127,614,000 | 2.26% |
| 3 | Germany | 861,500 | 81,802,000 | 2.02% |
| 4 | China | 477,400 | 1,341,000,000 | 0.06% |
| 5 | United Kingdom | 448,100 | 62,041,708 | 0.77% |
| 6 | France | 383,000 | 65,821,885 | 0.68% |
| 7 | Canada | 251,300 | 34,404,000 | 1.11% |
| 8 | Switzerland | 222,000 | 7,782,900 | 3.23% |
| 9 | Italy | 179,000 | 60,605,053 | 0.37% |
| 10 | Australia | 173,600 | 22,607,000 | 0.79% |
| 11 | Brazil | 146,700 | 190,732,694 | 0.09% |
| 12 | Spain | 143,000 | 46,152,925 | 0.32% |
| 13 | India | 139,835 | 1,210,193,422 | 0.01% |

*Source: Capgemini (a consultancy) and Merrill Lynch (a bank).*[2]

Did you know more than 90% of today's millionaires come from middle-income families? In *The New York Times* best-selling book, *The Millionaire Next Door, the Surprising Secrets of America's Wealthy*, author and researcher Dr. Thomas J. Stanley surveyed and conducted personal interviews with 500 U.S. millionaires over two decades. He used this data to reveal the secrets for building wealth in America.

---

2   Population Reference Bureau, *2009 World Population Data Sheet* (Washington DC: Population Reference Bureau, 2009)

Dr. Stanley concluded a person's economic background had little to do with his or her ability to become a millionaire. During his research, he found less than 10% of millionaires came from wealthy families. In *The Millionaire Next Door*, Dr. Stanley shattered the contemporarily held beliefs about how America's rich got that way. Inheritance, advanced degrees, or even intelligence does not always build fortunes in this country. Wealth in America is more often the result of hard work, diligent savings, and living below one's means. *The Millionaire Next Door* reveals the common denominators that repeatedly show up among those who have accumulated wealth.[3]

What makes this 3% so different from the rest of us? After reading books, researching, and attending seminars, I have come to realize it is a millionaire mindset that sets these folks apart. They simply were taught millionaire skills that have served and propelled them to success. These millionaire skills are learned; they are *not* inherited.

---

3     Thomas J. Stanley and William Danko, *The Millionaire Next Door, The Surprising Secrets of America's Wealthy* (New York, New York: Pocket Books, 1996)

## *What Millionaires Have in Common*

Millionaires all seem to have four common characteristics that drive them:

| Millionaire Mindset |
| :---: |
| Outlook |
| Attitude |
| Skills |
| Action |

These characteristics can be fostered in anyone, and who better to learn them than our kids.

In this book, I have taken these common characteristics and boiled them down to six millionaire skills—or ways of thinking—which every kid can and should learn:

| Millionaire Skills |
| :---: |
| Dream It |
| Believe It |
| Love It |
| Work It |
| Own It |
| Give It |

These six millionaire skills have become our family mottos. I found the most effective way to teach them to Jack by accident. I helped him start his own business and the skills just fell into place, like pieces of a puzzle.

If you make the effort to help your kid start a business, you will show them—in a very personal way—they can succeed in any environment. They will learn *they have it in them* to find a need and fill it. They can be a millionaire many times over if they have the desire and a "millionaire mindset." You will teach them the secret to success that only 3% of our population knows. You will teach them failure is not the end of the world but just a setback. They will know in their hearts they can do it over again. You will teach them the only formula they need for achievement:

"Dream It" + "Believe It" + "Love It" + "Work It" + "Own It" + "Give It" = Success

In this book, I will take you on an honest, step-by-step journey, describing what I did with Jack. You will have the benefit of learning from my mistakes. You will see just how easy it can be to teach these millionaire skills. Know this: you can help your kid start their own business regardless of whether you have owned your own business or not. I will also outline many of the wonderful life lessons Jack has learned and is still learning from this experience.

Perhaps most importantly, this book will teach you how to temper this growth in independence with compassion. It will be your job to show your child, when you have the ability to make money, you also have the responsibility to give back. You can help them learn rewards come in all forms, and you can teach them it is not always "just about the money".

It is important to understand what drove me to begin this journey with Jack, so I'll give you a brief background. At the end of Jack's second grade year, we decided to try a new school—a private school—one with a more developmental approach to learning.

At first, we thought the school was great. Jack seemed to like it and adjusted well. Then, about two months into it, I picked him up from school one afternoon and he burst into tears. He told me the kids were *mean* to him. His dad and I tried to be objective, you know, the "kids will be kids" thing. We tried not to jump to conclusions, but the truth is; over the next several months, Jack experienced bullying from about six of the boys in his class, and it got progressively worse. In the end, it became physical and violent.

We met with the principal and the teacher, who told us they knew they had a bullying problem—not just in our classroom but throughout the school. They were "working on it" and were interviewing bully consultants to help them implement a no-tolerance policy to teach the kids and improve the culture at the school. Who knew there was such a thing as a "bully consultant"?

The problem did not go away and the teacher could not control it. The teacher and the principal finally told us to talk to the parents of the bullies directly, so one morning, my husband John went to the mother of one of the boys who was bullying Jack. He tried to talk to her about the situation as the teacher had suggested. Her response was amazing.

She literally said, "I can't control how he treats his sister at home! What makes you think I can control him while he is at school?"

It went downhill from there. The bullying got worse and Jack was always on edge. The wonderful, happy-go-lucky boy we had known was gone.

I read every book I could find on bullying. In late spring, we had another meeting with the teacher and the principle, about six weeks or so before school was over. We asked when the bully consultant would begin. They said they decided not to hire anyone. They decided they did not have a problem and Jack did things to *deserve* the bullying. I was dumbfounded.

I got up from the meeting, told them we were finished, and took Jack out of the school. The immediate nightmare was over for Jack, but it took about nine months to a year before he was anywhere close to his old self again. His confidence and self-esteem was at an all-time low. He was a broken boy.

While this was going on, Jack was struggling with reading. He was not reading at grade level and in the back of my mind I feared Jack was dyslexic, so we had him tested. Sure enough, like me, he was diagnosed with Dyslexia. It was a blessing and a curse to know what was behind the reading problems. From my own childhood, I knew what it was like to live with Dyslexia. I knew firsthand the hit a kid's self-esteem could take in school when you could not read the simplest of paragraphs. I did not want that for Jack, but not wanting it was not going to wish it away.

We decided (I guess, looking back now, I really decided) to look into homeschooling. I researched and found a wonderful, easy-to-follow homeschool curriculum for Dyslexics called Verticy Learning[4]. I began homeschooling Jack for fourth grade. The curriculum was great and we could really see Jack progressing. I have to tell you, while homeschooling was a wonderful experience for both Jack and me, it was one of the hardest things I have ever done. I have such respect for those who homeschool their kids; man is it a commitment and a true act of love!

I also started thinking, "What can I do to help him build some self-esteem back?" The bully experience had taken a huge toll on Jack. If you have even known anyone who was bullied they will tell you, it is devastating. Add the bullying to the Dyslexia and I had one downtrodden boy on my hands. I knew I had to do something. It had to be something he could call his own, something that would be a success. He needed a win.

---

4    Verticy Learning, 10713 Gilroy Road, Suite B - Hunt Valley, MD 21031, 1-888-544-7116, www.verticylearning.org

I toyed with the idea of helping him start his own business. The more I thought about it, the more I was sure it would make a great start. I floated the idea by Jack, but he was less than thrilled with the prospect. I knew the business would help so I worked on him pretty hard. When he finally relented and said "Yes", I sprung into action. We were off and running! In coming chapters, I'll tell you more details about how we got started, but suffice to say, the millionaire seeds were planted and were starting to grow!

## The Title of this Book

The advice of those in the publishing game was to come up with a short catchy title. My first thought was to title the book: *How to raise a capable kid who can find their way out of a paper bag, by teaching them all the things they will never learn in school*, but that certainly was not short and it was not even *close* to catchy—clearly, it did not cut it.

It was Alex Carroll, author of *Beat the Cops*[5] who gave me the title. I loved it, but it has not been without its detractors. I found some people upon hearing the title ask, "So is Jack a millionaire?" It was clear to me; they did not understand the point of the book. I was really struggling.

Why weren't they getting it? It was a fellow author who came to my rescue. Mary Francis, author of a wonderful book called *The Sisterhood of Widows*[6] and a good friend gave me some sage advice. She suggested I keep the catchy title but make it clear in the subtitle I was talking about teaching kids millionaire skills. So I decided on *How to Raise a Millionaire: Six millionaire skills parents can teach their kids so they can imagine and live the life of their dreams!*

This book will give you the ideas and a roadmap anyone can use to teach their children to be capable, self-sufficient and handle difficult situations. It will help you show them just how wonderful passion and drive can be. It will help you teach them how to confidently take action.

We all want our kids to believe they can do anything they put their minds to do. This book will help you show them they can. We all know actions speak louder than words. This book will help you teach them what it takes to run their own business. If they end up working for someone else—as most people do—they will be one of the few employees who possess a firsthand understanding of the challenges their bosses face every day. This book will give you the tools you need to teach responsibility, dedication, attention to detail, and independence—all characteristics any boss would love to have in their employees.

Help your kid start a business and you will be well on your way to "raising a capable kid who can find their way out of a paper bag"—and maybe even a millionaire!

## *Jack's Book*

Once I decided to write the book, I knew I needed to educate myself about the book industry and what it would take for me to become a successful author.

*Meet Jack*

5    Alex Carroll, *Beat the Cops: The Guide to Fighting Your Traffic Ticket and Winning* (Santa Barbara, California: AceCo Publishers, 2001)

6    Mary Francis, *The Sisterhood of Widows: Sixteen True Stories of Grief, Anger and Healing* (New York, New York: Morgan James Publishing, 2011)

It was at one of these conferences where it hit me: I can write a book about how adults can help their kids, but that is only half the equation. It occurred to me Jack could write a book for kids to read. He could tell them about his experience and give them encouragement "kid-to-kid". I went home and asked Jack what he thought and he loved the idea! We spent a weekend mapping out his book and then he wrote it.

As I explained earlier Jack has Dyslexia, so I didn't want the writing process itself to hamper his creativity. I wanted him to do nothing but create, so I was his secretary, typing each word as he dictated it. All he had to do was create the outline and dictate the book! He did an amazing job.

We sent it off to some friends and asked for feedback. We incorporated their feedback and sent it to the book editor—grammatical errors and all. My hope was the editor would preserve his voice and she did! Jack's book is a great companion to mine; they dovetail nicely, and yet each can stand alone.

Jack's current goal is to become one of the youngest, best-selling authors on *The New York Times Best Seller List*, and I have no doubt he will get there! Why? Because Jack is able to "Dream It", "Believe It", "Love It", "Work It", "Own It" and "Give It"! When you buy his book for your kids to read, be sure to read his mission at the end of the book. During one of the seminars we attended, Jack wrote his mission. It still takes my breath away that my son has such a powerful mission in life. I have no doubt he will achieve his mission! I'll bet your kids have an equally stunning mission in life. It is your job to help them "Dream It", "Believe It"," Love It", "Work It", "Own It" and "Give It"!

> When Jack went through his horrific experience with bullying, I read a number of resources that helped me. There was no definitive source or reference because each situation is different. I got valuable nuggets from a number of different authors, website, etc.
>
> I hope if you find yourself in the situation where your son or daughter is being bullied these reference and resources are helpful to you.
>
> Remember, you are not alone. Together we can stop this trend dead in its tracks!
>
> **www.howtoraiseamillionaire.com/bully**

When Kevin Coffey and I first started collaborating on the illustrations for this book we worked to come up with an image to epitomize my feelings about the opportunities we can foster and encourage in our children as we raise them.

It is our responsibility to lift up our kids.
It is our responsibility to give our kids a hand.
It is our responsibility to give our kids a safe place to fail.
It is our responsibility to give our kids a nourishing place to grow.

This illustration is meant to symbolize these opportunities and responsibilities. As you read this book, you'll see the kids in the chapter illustrations climb. Like the kids in the illustrations, your kids can climb to success with your help and encouragement. In this book, the word *raise* means much more than just bringing our kids to maturity. It means to awaken, to arouse, to stir up, to incite, to lift up, to place higher, to elevate, to heighten, to invigorate, to cultivate and to grow.

Jack and I are on a mission. We want to fill the world with kid entrepreneurs. We want to give kids the practical tools and encouragements they need to build a future they can bank on—no matter what the economy throws their way.

**howtoraiseamillionaire.com**

*Chapter 1*

# Why Raise a Kid Entrepreneur?

*It is paradoxical that many educators and parents still differentiate between a time for learning and a time for play without seeing the vital connection between them.*

—*Leo F. Buscaglia*

## *The Information Age*

Entrepreneurs are not born; they are taught. Any kid—regardless of who their parents are, where or how their parents or others are raising them, and what the world around them offers—can be taught to think like a businessperson.

Our world has changed and we are smack dab in the middle of it. The world of our parents—going to work for one company, staying there all your adult life, and then retiring—is gone.

On the off chance you missed it, we have moved to the "Information Age." Automation and cheaper overseas labor have taken jobs once performed by people in this country. Pensions are shrinking and will soon be either gone or insignificant.

Retirement accounts are becoming obsolete. When our kids reach an age where they will want to stop working, the likelihood is, unless they planned properly, they will have little or no safety net. Self-directed individual retirement accounts or other retirement options will likely be commonplace. The middle class is disappearing before our eyes. In short, you will not be able to depend on your employer to provide a cushy retirement package so you can sail off into the sunset.

On top of that, competition for college—and college fees—are at an all-time high. Does anyone think those fees will come down anytime soon? It simply is not going to happen. In fact, we will see an even greater level of competition among our kids who are trying to get into colleges and universities. More and more kids will graduate from our universities with wonderful degrees only to enter a world with fewer jobs waiting for them.

They will need to stand out from the competition by showing a breadth of life experience and extracurricular activities like never before. Being an "A" student is not going to open the doors as it once did.

## Paths to Success

> *Your children need your presence more than your presents.*
>
> —*Jesse Jackson*

I have always been a "glass is half-full" person, so saying these things go against my nature; however, I am also practical. These statements are true about our society. We need to embrace them and retool our lives—and the lives of our kids—so we are all prepared for the world in which we live.

I wrote this book to provide parents a path to lead their kids to success. I designed it to help you sculpt your children so they have every possible advantage to build the life of their dreams. It is my passion because I see only blue skies ahead for our kids! I wanted my child to be capable, confident, and prepared for life.

Here are some questions I asked myself:

- What is going to help Jack stand out from the crowd?
- What is going to help him succeed in life?
- What can I do today to give him the practical skills he will need to go straight to the top of the list, regardless of what *list* he chooses?

- How can I help him overcome the damage the bullies did to his self-esteem?
- How can I help him deal with his challenges of Dyslexia and see there is success at the end of the struggle if he can just hang on?
- What can I do now to give him wins and make him feel good about himself?

These questions led me to the idea of helping him start his own business. I knew Jack learned best when he did things himself. I knew, if I could get him to start his own business, he would learn principles from the very act of starting the business that I could never teach him; however, I did not realize all the *extra* things he would learn along the way. I had thought the learning would be both tactical and strategic business skills but was astonished at the breadth of life skills Jack learned. I began to realize I was teaching him millionaire skills! I knew I was on to something big and each step we took together it became apparent just how big!

Nine months after Jack started his business, my husband asked for a divorce. I had my own successful marketing business, which I had started in 1997, but a year earlier, one of my steady clients—for the lack of a better word—laid me off and I no longer had a robust client list. I had not really gone out to get new work because, at the time, I had begun to homeschool Jack.

When my husband asked for the divorce, things changed. I found myself with no job, a son I homeschooled, and three dogs under the age of one. I immediately set out to determine the best course of action. I decided to revive a product I had been working on and started to attend seminars and classes to give me the skills I would need to sell it. I needed to succeed in my new life. With a change in career direction, I knew enough to know I didn't know enough! So I rolled up my sleeves and started studying.

I uncovered new marketing skills and brushed up on some old ones. I had the dream, the drive, and the ambition; I felt as if I could do whatever I set my mind to do. I began to realize I was dusting off my "millionaire mindset"—outlook, attitude, skills, and action. My parents taught my brother and me those skills. I had put those skills on the back burner for a few years and let the challenges of a dying marriage and home life start to snuff them out. I needed to give them a little attention to bring them back to life.

As I was teaching Jack how to start his own business, it suddenly dawned on me I was watching him learn those same millionaire skills—the ones my parents had taught me. By starting his own business, I had unwittingly set him on the path to learn outlook, attitude, skills, and action!

The more I saw what Jack was learning from the experience of starting his own business, the more convinced I became I had actually hit on something profound. The full impact of what I was doing—and what other parents could do—started to become something tangible. I realized my passion was to get this message out to other parents and adults. I began to focus on it and, before I knew it, the vehicle for my passion—this book—started to become a reality and take shape!

The millionaire skills Jack was learning needed to become lessons, so I went back to what I saw Jack learning and put it into words: "Dream It", "Believe It", "Love It", "Work It", "Own It" and "Give It".

Answering the question "Why?" seemed the logical place to start for this book. I realized it might not be obvious why someone should take the time to help their kid start a business. Why make this effort? Some of the results would probably seem obvious, but others—like the millionaire skills—would take a little explaining.

First let's start at another "W" question: *When.* We'll go greater into detail about *why* later in this chapter and you'll understand the extreme values behind empowering your kids with millionaire skills. You'll see how helping them start a business will make the task of teaching those skills a breeze.

Anyone can start this process with *any kid* at *any age.* However, I am often asked, "What is the perfect age?" My answer is, ideally, to start when your kids are in the fourth to eighth grades because between ages 7 through 13, kids are still impressionable. They take in what adults say and—for the most part—believe them. Let's face it; our credibility—their perception of the number of brain cells we possess—is on a rocket sled straight to you-know-where once they hit puberty. In short, your useful days are numbered!

## *The Greatest Lies You Will Tell Yourself*

> *The people you guys (parents) pay are spending more time with us (your kids) than you do!*
>
> —*Jack James*

There are a million (pun intended!) reasons why you should teach your kid millionaire skills and help your kid start their own business. For every reason you can think of to do it, there will be an equal number of reasons why you will not:

- "I don't have time."
- "My kid is already involved in _____ (insert any of the following: sports, music lessons, dancing lessons, etc.)."
- "You would not believe how much homework my kid has! We just don't have time."
- "I have never owned my own business. I don't know how to do it."
- "I can't do this. It is too hard."

- "I am not sure it will even work."
- "My kid won't listen to me."

Have I made a good start? These are all valid arguments but not showstoppers, unless *you* make them showstoppers. I want to spend a little time discussing why you should make the extra effort required and invest your time in your kid.

I am the worst procrastinator in the world—the worst! I can always think of more reasons why I should not do something than why I should. However, helping Jack start, grow and continue his business and teaching him a millionaire mindset was not one of the things I ever questioned doing. Maybe it was because—deep down inside—I could see the benefits even before they happened.

If you are ready to get started, skip this chapter. There is no reason to listen to me yammer about why you should do this. Congratulations, you are already drinking from the cup! However, if you are on the fence and you already have an internal dialog about all the things you should, would or could do rather than help your kid this way, read on.

Parenting is not easy. There is no doubt "giving in" to our kids is the path of least resistance and a lot easier, but that path is a complete disservice to our kids. They need structure. They crave boundaries. When we set boundaries and structure we have to stick to them, we can't cave. When you say, "I don't have the time," I understand. We all have school, homework, sports, music lessons, and other activities filling up our week.

The Bureau of Labor Statistics reports, in households with children ages 6 through 17, adults **on average** spend 47 minutes a day providing primary child care.[7] *Forty-seven minutes a day!* Be honest and ask yourself this question: "How much *quality* time do I actually spend with my kid, excluding doing homework, feeding them, driving them here and there, etc?" I had to be honest with myself and, while it is more than 47 minutes a day, it was not a huge amount. When I honestly looked at it, it made me rather sad.

Now ask yourself this question: "Do I want my child to have every possible skill they need to be a success in life?" If the answer is yes, then you need to spend time helping them learn the six millionaire skills I have outlined in this book! The easiest way I know for anyone to put those skills into education action is by helping their kid start their own business.

Most of us take our kids to paid tutors, music teachers, sports coaches and other folks hoping those people will be able to mold our kids into well rounded individuals. The truth is they learn from us every day, every minute we are with them. By making the effort to spend a focused one hour a week with them so they can start and run a business, they will learn skills those paid professional and wonderful volunteers just can't teach them. Period.

## *Bully-proofing Self-esteem and Handling Rejection Are Just Parts of Life*

> *It ain't what they call you, it's what you answer to.*
>
> *—W.C. Fields*

*Merriam-Webster* defines "self-esteem" as "a confidence and satisfaction in oneself,"[8] which may be misleading and confused with "self-conceit". Self-esteem is crucial to children because it defines their attitudes about themselves and, in my mind, is one of the cornerstones of a positive attitude towards life. It affects how we think, act and relate to other people. Raising a child with good self-esteem will help them live life to their potential. On the opposite

7    United States Department of Labor, Bureau of Labor Statistic ,*Care of Household Children(by Adults in Households with Children)*, (United States Department of Labor, Washington, DC, June 2011).

8    Merriam-Webster Online Dictionary, Springfield, MA 2011 by Merriam-Webster, Incorporated

side of the coin, raising a kid with low self-esteem means they will wrestle with negative thoughts about themselves, so each win will be an uphill battle.

# Confidence Coins

Why is it so hard to remember to compliment our kids? I found myself making corrections to Jack's behavior often and I was forgetting to give him the positive encouragement he needed. I learned this trick a long time ago when I started as a cub scout leader. This technique has really helped me learn to make sure the positives far outweigh the negatives.

Here is the trick. Put 10 coins in your left pocket when you start the day. Throughout the day, find positive things to say to your kids. Things like:

"Thanks for helping me this morning by getting ready without me having to nag you. It really makes my life easier and I appreciate it."

"I love when you start your homework without me having to ask, Thanks!"

"You were so nice to your sister today. Thanks for being a good brother."

"You look nice today, I love that shirt on you."

Each time you say something encouraging, nice or thank your kid, move one coin over to your right pocket. Here comes the hard part. No corrections or negative feedback until all the coins are in your right pocket.

The experts tell us by the time our kids are six years old, they have heard negative feedback over 40,000 times. "Don't do this", "don't do that"; think about it, I am sure I am guilty. I know I am far from perfect, but this trick has helped me become a more positive and uplifting parent to my son! Give it a try, you'll love the results!

Most things do not come easily; they require work and effort. If we do not arm our kids with a healthy dose of self-esteem, the work life requires can become overwhelming and they may find it simply easier to give up.

A few years ago, I heard a country western song *Sounds like life to me* sung by Darryl Worley. The song is about a guy whose friend has fallen off the wagon. The friend's wife calls, asking him to go to the bar where she knows her husband will be. The guy goes to the bar and finds his friend drinking. His friend starts telling him how nobody understands his troubles—his rent is due, the kids need shoes, the dishwasher broke and so on. He gives his friend a list of reasons why it is okay for him to be in a bar, drinking away his problems. The chorus (and point) of the song is simply, "Sounds like life to me."

My only point in referencing this song is that life is a series of situations we must learn how to handle. We need to teach our kids how to get through the rough patches and keep their self-esteem intact. It is our job as parents to help them understand we cannot let ordinary life derail and overwhelm us.

We have to find a way to overcome the obstacles we encounter and move past them. So many of the activities in which our kids are involved these days are set up to be "fair"; too many of us work very hard to prevent our kids from "losing".

Life requires work and effort. You have to get out of bed, go to work and pay the bills. Whether you are Donald Trump, Bill Gates, a garden-variety business professional or a tradesperson you still have to get out of bed and go to work. We all need the stuff it takes to get past the hard times. If our self-esteem is only high when we are winning, what happens when we do not win? What happens when life throws us a curve? Worse yet, if our self-esteem tells us we are not worthy, guess what? We will never allow ourselves to be in the position *to* win. Teaching our kids how to win *and* lose is equally important; in fact, learning how to lose teaches our kids an even greater lesson. We are teaching the true lesson of self-esteem: self-worth is about how we react when we win *or* lose.

I am an archery range master and for the past several summers, I have taught archery to Cub Scouts at day camp. Each camp session has an average of about 120 kids. One year, per my usual routine, I had arranged an archery contest at the end of the week. There were prizes for the top archers in camp, as well as opportunities for first, second, and third place in each of the dens. (A greater number of categories meant more kids could be winners!) I like to teach achievement camps where the kids are divided by age. By adding the top archers per den, I made it possible for the younger kids to be winners too. When you add it all up; the three awards for each age group plus the three overall winners makes a total of about 39 awards possible.

I asked the camp director (a new guy that year) for the camper list so I could make up certificates for each scout, (everybody goes home with a fun archery certificate). I also needed to make sure I had a list for the competition. I was dumbfounded when the director told me "they" would not allow a shooting contest. He went on to explain "they" did not want any of the boys to feel bad if they did not win. He also explained "we" did not do things in Cub Scouts to exclude boys in *that* way. Clearly, I was not a "they" or a "we".

I was floored. What an utter disservice to our children! Mind you, he was in charge of the camp, so I gave him no argument about not doing the shooting competition (frankly, it saved me a lot of extra work), but give me a break! One of the biggest events in any Cub Scout pack around the United States—and probably around the world—is the Pinewood Derby. This is an annual activity where the boys build wooden race cars with adult assistance and race them down pinewood tracks for *prizes and trophies*. A number of other youth groups have emulated this fun event. In 1953, Don Murphy, a Cubmaster from Manhattan Beach, California, who organized the first Pinewood Derby, said this about the worldwide phenomenon he started:

> "I wanted to devise a wholesome, constructive activity that would foster a closer father-son relationship and promote craftsmanship and good sportsmanship through competition."[9]

I do not think Don's vision of derbies included an "everyone has to be a winner" clause. We have gotten so far off the track (pun intended) with this politically correct stuff we have forgotten what our world is really like.

Life is a competition. We compete for jobs. We compete for college admission. We compete in sports. We compete for significant others. We compete when we buy a house (OK I live in California, where bids over the asking price are still in fashion, despite a down turned economy). In our zeal to make sure our kids never feel the pain of losing we have thrown out the baby with the bathwater. In our haste to make sure our kids only feel like *winners*, we have neglected to teach them gracious defeat. We have stopped teaching our kids how to be resilient, how to overcome a setback and how to handle the word "No". We have to teach our kids how to bounce back from failure on their own. We have to teach our kids to believe in themselves and their dreams because they have to be able to overcome a lot of obstacles on their journey to success. If we teach them to "Dream It", but not to "Believe It", they will never *make it*.

Nearly every millionaire has lost their fortune or a part of it at some time in their career. Regardless of how it was lost, I would bet each one could build

---

9    Don Murphy, *Pinewood! The Story of the Pinewood Derby*, (Cambridge England, Perfect Paperback, 2001) Don Murphy, Founder of the Pinewood Derby in 1953, Manhattan Beach, CA Cub Scout Pack 280C.

their business back in a couple of years to be better than it was before. Why? It is simple; they know how to recover from setbacks. They know setbacks are a part of life and business, and they do not let them color their world. They have faith in themselves. They know how to "Believe It!"

Every time we let our kids fall and we pick them up, dust them off and let them start over again, we are giving them a push down the road to healthy self-esteem and healthy resilience. We are teaching them a key ingredient to one of the six millionaire skills.

An amazing young woman named Kristi O'Donnell worked for me. She was a strong, self-assured, remarkable person. I am using past tense because she sadly passed away from ovarian cancer at the age of 33.

She was an athlete, a scholar and an accomplished artist in her mid-twenties when she came to work for me. While God certainly had a hand in making Kristi the unique gift she was, I am sure the success she experienced in her short life was—in part—due to her parents, Dennis (O'D) and Barbara O'Donnell.

She told me her dad was quite a driving force in her life. Starting when she was very young, he coached, taught and guided her through the ups and downs of her childhood. The policy in their house was—unless there was blood—whenever you fell, you did not fuss, cry or carry on. Instead, you pretended falling was "a part of the act". He taught her to literally get up, spread her arms and say, "Ta-da!"

It might seem silly but, at the time she told me this story, Jack was very small and I thought it was quite wise. Even at a young age, her father taught her to roll with the punches. When life knocks you down, you get back up. Kristi was taught you do not sit there, look at your boo-boo, cry and wait for someone to come and make it all better or rescue you.

O'D could not have known how well this life skill would serve Kristi when she battled cancer at the age of 24. She had more grace and courage than anyone I have ever known.

## Teaching How to Not Take Rejection Personally

While you are helping your kids learn the ropes of starting a business, *never* lose sight of the greater goal—those millionaire skills they are learning. They are learning—through osmosis—lessons that will serve them for the rest of their lives and they do not even know it! You are teaching them, and it is fun!

Part of starting a business is about asking people to buy your product or service. The hardest part of sales is rejection. Your kid is probably going to ask 20 to 30 neighbors to buy their product or service before one says "Yes". *Did you hear me?* Twenty people are going to listen to your adorable kid's spiel and tell them, "No, thanks."

You are going to have to stand there, let your kid get all tongue-tied, stop and start, say only half of what you rehearsed, get embarrassed— and you will say *nothing*. You are going to do this knowing there is every likelihood, at the end of it, your neighbor will tell them "No". In short, you are going to help your little darling learn to look at the twenty times they hear "No" as twenty "Not at this time". In our household "No" has come to mean "Next".

You are going to teach your kids to "Dream It", "Believe It" and "Love It" so much that when someone tells them they are not interested in what they are selling, their "Love It" millionaire skill kicks in and they move undaunted to the "Next" potential customer. I have to warn you, once you teach your kids "No means Next" and how to ask—which is covered a little later in this chapter and again in chapter two because it is so important—you'll be in for a fun ride. They will start using the tools they are learning on *you*!☺

Rejection—for not getting the raise, the job, the date, the house or the part in the play—is part of the game of life. You are teaching your child to cope with the negative without having it devastate them and trash their self-esteem. Honestly, there is no greater gift to give our children than to be able to handle rejection as a part of life. Is it going to be hard? *Absolutely!* It is one of the hardest gifts for parents to give—but one of the most important.

Where else is self-esteem useful? In school? A kid's self-esteem is so very important—and definitely at risk—in school. In his work, *America's Lost Dream*, James W. Prescott, PhD, sites alarming statistics of which we should all be aware:

> "Depression and suicide are of epidemic proportions in America. Suicide has been the third leading cause of death in the youth age group of 15–24 years for the past generation (1979–1997) and is the fifth and sixth leading cause of death in the 5–14 year age group for the years 1979 and 1997, respectively."[10]

I am 51 and from my generation to now, child suicides have tripled. *Tripled!* This is shocking but understandable when you think about how much we hear about bullies in our schools these days. When I was a kid, bullies teased me about being a redhead. It hurt and made elementary school unpleasant, but kids today deal with a lot worse. If we can help our kids develop bully-proof self-esteem, we will be giving them more needed tools in their arsenal to make it through middle and high school! I have seen first-hand what bullying can do.

---

10  James W. Prescott, PhD, *America's Lost Dream* (Lansing, NY: Institute of Humanistic Science, August 1, 2002) p. 32 Monthly Vital Statistics Report, Centers for Disease Control and Prevention/National Center for Health Statistics, "Advance Report of Final Mortality Statistics, 1994," Vol. 45, No. 3, Supplement, September 30, 1996 (Tables 6 & 7)

It took Jack a long time to overcome the hurt. He is still very sensitive to what others think about him and we work on it constantly.

This self-esteem building starts with learning to take rejection for what it is: something that happens in everyday life; something you cannot take personally; something from which you get over and walk away! It *sounds like life* to me!

I have to admit, I can't remember any parent ever saying to me, "Yep, I sure love it when my kid is hurt!" We all want to protect our children from hurt and disappointment but, in the process, we are overlooking this fact; hurt and disappointment are part of life. We need to prepare and teach our kids how to deal with it gracefully and recover more strongly because of it. Teaching our kids to believe in their dreams and themselves are the millionaire skills that allow them to have something to love. When they "Love It", it is easier for them to look past other people's opinions and put-downs. It allows them to push past the negatives and see the positives.

## Teaching Confidence without Being Cocky

> *"You don't raise heroes, you raise sons. And if you treat them like sons, they'll turn out to be heroes, even if it's just in your own eyes."*
>
> —*Walter Schirra, Sr.*

There is a difference between being "confident" and being "cocky". Once your child decides to start a business and gets a customer or two, you will see them begin to develop a new kind of confidence. They will see the "Dream It", "Believe It" and "Love It" millionaire skills turn fruitful and you know what, it feels really good! Your job will be to help keep this newly found self-confidence from turning into cockiness.

As they build their business and have success, they will become more and more aware of their capabilities and will naturally become more confident, but they will need to learn to be humble about it. Having confidence in yourself and letting others know you are confident in yourself are two different things. Our kids need to learn to be humble in success just as much as they need to learn to be gracious in setbacks.

Rennu Dhillon is the founder of a San Francisco Bay Area program called Genius Kids, which helps kids learn to be capable. Dhillon says,

> "Instilling self-confidence in a child will impact their entire life. Self-confident people will have better relationships with family, friends, and work associates. They are able to set attainable goals and make better decisions in their personal and professional life."[11]

Dhillon has devoted her life's work to help raise capable kids. She strongly endorses the fact that, in order to survive in today's fast-paced and ever-changing world, we need to create confident, happy, and successful citizens who will become future leaders. In her article, *How to Teach Children Self-Confidence and Self-Worth*, Dhillon gives us the following guidelines, which I think are brilliant:

> **Teach kids to think for themselves**—children need to learn to develop their own critical thinking skills so encourage your child to figure out answers. If the child is taking longer than you expect them to answer a question, it is okay. As parents we get frustrated and give the answer to them. This does not help. Encourage them to think and come up with an answer of their own. If the answer is correct or even partially correct, applaud and praise them, if the answer is incorrect, explain to them why

it is incorrect and praise them for trying to participate. Children learn by the action of doing.

**Teach kids the importance of practical knowledge**—being street smart is as important as being book smart. If children learn how to do things by themselves with actual practical experience, they will become more confident in their abilities.

Example: Coloring—many kids like to scribble on their homework and it is easier for the parent to finish off the coloring page and move on to something else. Have your child take pride in their work and praise them when they complete the task properly.

**Share as many stories as possible**—Children love to hear stories and sharing your experiences with them will help them relate better to you. Effective open communication is the key to a healthy relationship between parents and children. Children feel more comfortable when they can believe that their parents have had similar experiences to themselves, especially in challenging situations such as being bullied at school.

**If you at first don't succeed, try again**—an important belief to instill in every child. Everyone faces failure at some time or another in their life and some things take longer to grasp than others. Teach your child to accept their failures as an experience and a reason to try again and become better. In school competitions and events, teach the spirit of participation rather than winning. Children should be taught that not everyone can win or come first but everyone can participate and try to win.

**Develop the strengths**—when growing up children are under immense pressure of excelling in all subjects at school. It is important to teach kids to do their best in all the subjects but to maximize themselves in the areas they excel in. In this way children will develop confidence-becoming experts in certain areas instilling confidence in their abilities.

**Etiquette and Manners**—instilling etiquette and manners from a young age and teaching children how to behave in a social gathering interacting with other people is very important. Ensure that your child plays with different groups of children and help them learn to make friends by encouraging play dates at your home.

Instilling self-confidence in a child will impact their entire life. People who are self-confident will have better relationships with family, friends and work associates. They are able to set attainable goals and make better decisions in their personal and professional life.[11]

The very fact your kid will be starting their own business will begin to build the confidence you are seeking. The trick is to help keep them humble.

## Teaching Responsibility

> *"If you want children to keep their feet on the ground, put some responsibility on their shoulders."*
> —*Abigail Van Buren*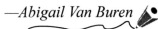

Parents want their kids to be responsible. I have spent countless hours talking, cajoling, begging and—yes—screaming at Jack to be more responsible. I

---

11   Rennu Dhillon, *How to Teach Children Self-Confidence and Self-Worth,* (Fremont, CA: Genius Kids, April 2009)

never dreamed the act of starting his own business would drive him to be responsible all on his own—no need for me to say one word! Perfect? No. Much better? Yes!

As parents, we have all found ourselves getting ready to walk out the door and hollering a list of things our kid needs to do, like "Brush your teeth! Put your shoes on! Grab your backpack!" How many of us have stood outside, ready to go and then—tired of waiting—gone back in the house only to find your kid in their room fiddling with something—no shoes on, teeth not brushed, and backpack unpacked? You look at them and they look back at you dumbstruck. What do you do? If you are like me, you lose it! Just ask Jack! ☺

If your kids are between the ages of 7 and 13, they are in "middle childhood," a critical time for kids. The bad news is they are just ready to jump off the cliff into puberty. The good news is—in their eyes—you still have a brain in your head.

Middle childhood is a time when kids can still develop a love for learning. Parents can still introduce the idea of starting their own business (*work*—that is) and they will get enthusiastic about it. If you think your child is too young, think again. The best time to begin the adventure of being a business owner is when they are in this wonderful, in-between world of *middle childhood*. Establishing any business takes time; they will not see results—read: money—right off the bat.

You will want to start and grow a business at an age where money is not the only thing that keeps them going.

If you ask an eight year old to help you cook dinner, they are thrilled—over the moon. They love the doing—they love being with you. If you ask a 10 year old to help you cook dinner, after a moment's hesitation, they are all in. If you ask a 16 year old to help you cook dinner, unless you have already made cooking dinner together a special time, helping you cook dinner is nothing short of work and they are not going to jump for joy. Middle childhood is the perfect time to introduce and teach our fourth millionaire skill, "Work It."

Kids ages 7 through 13 love the feeling of accomplishment for accomplishment's sake. There does not have to be an end goal or a benefit—if you will. The benefit is just doing the work itself, especially if it is with you. They will pick up on the thrill of the finish; "Work It" becomes an easy skill to master and it becomes its own reward. When they get a little older, they start to look at work as well...*work*. Work becomes something they do not want to do, unless there is an end goal in mind. If you wait until they are pre-teen, the benefits of the business—the money—will need to arrive more quickly for the business to hold their interest.

On the other hand, if the business is well in hand by the time they are pre-teens and moving into full-blown puberty, the benefits—read: *cold, hard cash*—will outweigh the costs—read: *the work*. The trick is to make sure—by the time they hit puberty—they have established their business and see the benefit of having extra cash in their pockets. In the magical time called middle childhood, achievements are still a motivating factor in and of themselves;

ultimately, these all play together to help develop competence, build confidence and grow their self-esteem. A well established "Work It" millionaire skill will survive the inevitable fountain of teenage hormones and will likely transfer very quickly and easily from the business to school work, just about the time things like GPA really start to matter.

The truth is kids ages 7 through 13 do not really need money. They might see something in a store or on television and decide they want it—you can use this to create an opportunity for goal setting and achievement—but in most cases, they will lose interest or just plain forget. When they are older and want to do things requiring cold hard cash, the business will provide them with the means to achieve their goals. These goals can be as simple as being able to go to the movies with friends on a Saturday night. You will not have to stress the benefits of running their business; the ability to fund their goals will do that for you.

Starting a business begins a huge cycle of responsibility they will have established between their customer and themselves. Time to understand something very important: this does not involve you. Believe it or not, this is the key! As kids, they sometimes disappoint or let down their parents, but letting down a customer, a teacher, a coach, or a scout leader, is a different matter entirely. This is why extracurricular activities are so critical to the development of young children; they are beholden to someone outside their family.

If we have done our job correctly from birth, our kids know from the inside out, we will provide them with unconditional love. They know we will love them no matter what. It is the double edge sword we wield as parents. It is what allows them to disappoint us at times. But teachers, clients, coaches and other adult leadership figures are a different matter. Their respect is earned and has to be kept.

In Chapter 3, I will give a specific example of how Jack's sense of responsibility to his clients is something I never had to teach him. He learned it himself—by doing.

## *Teaching How to Talk to Adults*

> *"Anyone who thinks the art of conversation is dead ought to tell a child to go to bed."*
>
> —*Robert Gallagher*

We have all met kids who did not know how to interact with adults. Maybe they are shy, look down at the floor when they are talking or do not answer questions unless someone, like their parent, says, "Junior! They asked you a question! Please answer them."

We all know kids who can rattle the windows with their voices when they are with their buddies. Then suddenly, when asked to interact with an adult, cannot be heard because they are barely speaking above a whisper. What happens? It is simple. No one has taught them how to speak to a stranger. We have all been so worried about teaching them *not* to talk to strangers we have forgotten most of our world *is* strangers! The grocery clerk, the mail carrier, the police officer, the firefighter and the ride operator at Disneyland are all strangers ... I could go on and on, but you get my drift. We need to teach our kids how to be smart when they are talking to a stranger. Most strangers are usually adults, so we need to teach our kids how to talk to them. This is another learned skill. It is not inherited and we have to teach them, just like we teach them to say "Please" and "Thank you".

I bet some of you are saying, "Hey, I've *told* them how to do it. They just don't do it!" Guess what? Part of learning is doing. Why do you think our kids get five hundred million math problems every night? It is because repetition is one of the tools of learning (or at least that is what teachers tell us—there is a point where repetition becomes reprehensible). If our kids have been told how to respectfully talk to adults, but are never given the chance to practice, how can we expect them to be able to remember how to do it? Practice is the key.

Before we launch into this discussion, let me make myself clear. I am not an expert in child safety or suggesting you instruct your kid to go around your neighborhood knocking on doors. You have to be smart and protective of your kid. I am saying we have to separate "talking with adults/strangers" from "stranger danger".

When I say, "talking to strangers", I am discussing how they would talk to the grocery clerk or the mail carrier. They are indeed strangers, but we need to teach children how to show adults and others respect.

Here are three things I taught Jack to do when he is talking to an adult:

1. Look them in the eye.
2. Listen to what they are saying to you.
3. Answer them politely when they ask you a question.

They are pretty simple, but simple is part of the key. Keeping it simple and practical is what they need. It is our job to find them safe opportunities and let them practice.

Learning how to communicate to adults is a skill that will serve your kids all their lives, because at some point they will be adults too. You are teaching them basic communication skills, something every millionaire and successful person can do. Communication skills are critical to the success of all six millionaire skills. They need to be able to articulate their dreams, both to themselves and others. They need to communicate their belief in their dreams. Nothing says I am serious better than eye contact! They need to communicate their enthusiasm with conviction and gravity. They need strong communication skills to work with and for other people. They need to have a strong voice when they take responsibility and lastly they need to be able to communicate with all people showing them grace and consideration. Communication is a key skill. It is a *learned* skill. When we give our kids the skills to speak to someone in a superior position with confidence and grace, we give them the tools they need to become the leaders of tomorrow.

# Making the Most of Drive Time

We listen to audio books when we are driving for a long time. Instead of giving Jack a movie to watch and not engage with me, we listen to a book together. Sometimes it is a children's novel, but we also listen to audio books from motivational speakers. We have listened to the The Aladdin Factor by Jack Canfield and Mark Victor Hansen,[7] and a number of other Canfield books.

When Jack hears someone else tell him about the power of positive thinking, it is different than when I tell him. It is not his mom nagging him; it is an authority figure. You do not have to break the bank either because the library is a great source for audio books.

Give it a try! You will fill dead travel time with great learning, and have something in common to discuss with your kids afterward. My guess is you will be hooked like we are! We laugh, have fun, enjoy each other's company and learn all at the same time! ☺

## *Teaching Kids How to Ask*

As you help your kid to start their own business, learning how to ask will be an amazing gift they will use over and over again in life. I know this may sound like a silly thing, but the art of asking is something we usually do not teach our kids—let alone learn ourselves. It sets successful people apart from the masses.

There are many reasons why people do not like to ask; one of the biggest being the fear of rejection. As children, we are taught not to ask about things that are not our business. We spend a lot of time as parents unintentionally teaching our kids NOT to ask.

> "Don't ask me for that."
> "If you ask me again, I swear, I don't know what I'll do."
> "Are you crazy? We can't afford that. Why do you even ask?"
> "You already know what the answer is. Why are you asking?"
> "The answer is No."

Sound familiar? I know it does for me. I have to constantly stop and fight the voices I hear inside my own head so I don't instantly react with a negative response, just because Jack asked. Teaching how to ask is hard, especially when it is hard for me.

Jack Canfield and Mark Victor Hansen have a great book about the art of asking called *The Aladdin Factor: Anything is possible - If you dare to ask!*[12] We have the audio version of the book. In the book, they suggest using The 8 Principles of Asking:

1. Ask as if you expect to get it
2. Ask with conviction
3. Ask someone who can give it to you
4. Be clear and specific
5. Ask from your heart
6. Ask with humor and creativity
7. Give in order to get
8. Ask repeatedly

---

12   Jack Canfield and Mark Victor Hansen, *The Aladdin Factor: Anything is possible - If you dare to ask!* (New York, NY, Macmillan Audio, 1995)

These eight steps might seem obvious to some but, if you are not good at asking for things, these principles can transform you from a paralyzed asker to an authentic asker—who gets what they want. However, forewarned is forearmed. Remember what I said, after you teach these principles and help your kid practice them, you might fall victim to their spell! Maybe Jack and Mark should write a book about answering "No"!☺

Once your child starts their own business, they will soon realize they need to master the art of asking. Help them try different techniques with their prospects. I will go into more detail in Chapter 2 about these principles and how asking factored into Jack's business.

As I mentioned before, Jack is a Boy Scout. Part of most youth programs involves some kind of fundraising. For many Boy Scout and Cub Scout units that means selling popcorn each year. It is a way for the kids to earn money for camp and other activities in their troops and packs.

In Jack's Boy Scout troop, we combined a fundraiser with an opportunity for the scouts to earn their Salesmanship Merit Badge. I am an Assistant Scoutmaster and a Merit Badge Counselor for Jack's troop. As such, I was putting on a presentation to the boys about sales. While searching for something inspirational about learning to ask, I found a wonderful story in one of the *Chicken Soup for the Soul*[13] books again by Jack Canfield and Mark Victor Hansen. Those two guys keep cropping up don't they!

---

13   Jack Canfield and Mark Victor Hansen, *Chicken Soup for the Soul, Ask, Ask, Ask* (the story of Markita Andrews) (Deerfield Beach, FL: Health Communications, Inc., 1993)

Here is the story, called *Ask, Ask, Ask,* I read to the boys and used as an example of how to ask:

> The greatest saleswoman in the world today doesn't mind if you call her a girl. That's because Markita Andrews has generated more than eighty thousand dollars selling Girl Scout cookies since she was seven years old.
>
> Going door-to-door after school, the painfully shy Markita transformed herself into a cookie-selling dynamo when she discovered, at age 13, the secret of selling.
>
> It starts with desire. Burning, white-hot desire.
>
> For Markita and her mother, who worked as a waitress in New York after her husband left them when Markita was eight years old, their dream was to travel the globe. "I'll work hard to make enough money to send you to college," her mother said one day. "You'll go to college and when you graduate, you'll make enough money to take you and me around the world. Okay?"
>
> So at age 13 when Markita read in her Girl Scout magazine that the Scout who sold the most cookies would win an all-expenses-paid trip for two around the world, she decided to sell all the Girl Scout cookies she could—more Girl Scout cookies than anyone in the world, ever.
>
> But desire alone is not enough. To make her dream come true, Markita knew she needed a plan.
>
> "Always wear your right outfit, your professional garb," her aunt advised. "When you are doing business, dress like you are doing business. Wear your Girl Scout uniform. When you go up to people in their tenement buildings at 4:30 or 6:30 and especially on Friday night, ask for a big order. Always smile, whether they buy or not, always be nice. And don't ask them to buy your cookies; ask them to invest."
>
> Lots of other Scouts may have wanted that trip around the world. Lots of other Scouts may have had a plan. But only Markita went off in her uniform each day after school, ready to ask—and keep asking—folks to invest in her dream. "Hi, I have a dream. I'm earning a trip around the world for me and my mom by

merchandising Girl Scout cookies," she'd say at the door. "Would you like to invest in one dozen or two dozen boxes of cookies?"

Markita sold 3,526 boxes of Girl Scout cookies that year and won her trip around the world. Since then, she has sold more than 42,000 boxes of Girl Scout cookies, spoken at sales conventions across the country, starred in a Disney movie about her adventure and has co-authored the best seller, *How to Sell More Cookies, Condos, Cadillacs, Computers ... And Everything Else.*

Markita is no smarter and no more extroverted than thousands of other people, young and old, with dreams of their own. The difference is Markita had discovered the secret of selling: Ask, Ask, Ask! Many people fail before they even begin because they fail to ask for what they want. The fear of rejection leads many of us to reject ourselves and our dreams long before anyone else ever has the chance—no matter what we're selling.

And everyone is selling something. "You're selling yourself everyday—in school, to your boss, to new people you meet," said Markita at 14. "My mother is a waitress: she sells the daily special. Mayors and presidents trying to get votes are selling ... I see selling everywhere I look. Selling is part of the whole world."

It takes courage to ask for what you want. Courage is not the absence of fear. It's doing what it takes despite one's fear. And, as Markita has discovered, the more you ask, the easier (and more fun) it gets.

Once, on live TV, the producer decided to give Markita her toughest selling challenge. Markita was asked to sell Girl Scout cookies to another guest on the show. "Would you like to invest in one dozen or two dozen boxes of Girl Scout cookies?" she asked.

"Girl Scout cookies? I don't buy any Girl Scout cookies!" he replied. "I'm a Federal Penitentiary warden. I put 2,000 rapists, robbers, criminals, muggers and child abusers to bed every night."

Unruffled, Markita quickly countered, "Mister, if you take some of these cookies. Maybe you won't be so mean and angry and evil. And, Mister, I think it would be a good idea for you to take some of these cookies back for every one of your 2,000 prisoners, too."

Markita asked.

The Warden wrote a check.

What a wonderful story to show the power of teaching kids to ask! Markita gave people a reason to want to help her by letting them know her goals. Once she told them her goal, she invited them into her world; she invited them to be a part of the process of reaching her goals. Some of us might want to buy the cookies just because they are good, but we all get satisfaction out of knowing the higher purpose of our purchase. This is a great lesson about the art of asking. It shows in a very real and tangible way how asking is a key component to several millionaire skills.

## *Learning How to Save and Reinvest Profits*

> *"We teach children to save their money. As an attempt to counteract thoughtless and selfish expenditure, that has value. But it is not positive; it does not lead the child into the safe and useful avenues of self-expression or self-expenditure. To teach a child to invest and use is better than to teach him to save."*
>
> *—Henry Ford*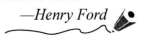

I taught Jack to put aside at least 70% of the income from his business; he can spend the other 30% on whatever he chooses. If he gets tips, he can spend those as well. I helped him open a savings account, and he is watching his bank account grow. The kid got an ATM card! How wild is that?? I guess you could look at it as dangerous, but the interesting thing is he saves it all! He never even uses the card, but the fact he has one is very cool to him. The decision to save it all is one he made on his own. Occasionally, he decides he needs or wants to buy something, but not very often. All the money he collects from his business goes into his bank account. I think he likes to see it grow. If we can't get to the bank right away, it goes in a special bag he keeps in his dresser—a zippered bank bag he got from his Uncle Buck. Easy to see why that bag is so darn special to Jack—it's from U.B.—who walks on water in both our eyes.

Remember: This is a journey. The next step in the journey is to reinvest some of those funds back into his business to help make it grow. Reinvesting might be in the form of marketing, buying a piece of equipment allowing him to offer other services or even the purchase of his referral gifts—such as Starbucks™ gift cards.

Jack and I discuss the next steps to grow his business: a key step to learning goal setting and goal achievement. I have made sure he does not grow his business any faster than he can handle it—physically and mentally. In the next chapter, I will talk more about how I did this.

If there is something your child wants to buy, have them take 10 or 15% of the profits and put it in another fund for the item. Let them work to save the money to buy the item. Remember, we are teaching many things here: business growth, reinvestment and impulse control. We are teaching not just buying whatever you see and want but making valued decisions and spending within your means. Responsibility and the proper handling of money is a basic principle your kids will need to learn to master the "Own It" millionaire skill. *Owning it* is taking responsibility regardless of whether the outcome is a good thing or a bad thing. Owning the bad things you do might just be more important than owning the good. It teaches character—a hard lesson indeed—but a necessary and valuable one.

You will need to help guide all these teaching moments, which can be very rewarding. It is also gratifying when your child buys an item and you watch them take good care of it. This is part of growing up and learning to properly take care of their things. It is surprising how much better Jack treats something when he's had to earn the money to pay for it.

If you are already paying allowance, or contemplating doing so, stop! Let me pause and say right here; if my views on allowance don't match yours, hear me out. On its face, allowance is a great tool, but we need to use it properly. Household responsibilities are just that: responsibilities. They are not—and should not be—jobs for which you are paid. I do not get paid to cook dinner or do the dishes, and I do not expect to pay my kid to do his share around the house. It is critical to assign tasks around the house to our kids; things they can do successfully like set the table, clear the table, fold and put away laundry or bring in the mail. Make helping around the house part of their responsibilities as a family member. It is equally important to remember to make the responsibilities a task within their developmental abilities. Do not give them a task at which they cannot succeed; give them a task where they can soar. If they forget easily, devise some chart, list or way to help them remember.

# What she'll be is up to me!

One of the challenges I faced as a family was getting my husband and Jack to help me around the house. I tried everything to get them both to do simple things like, pick up their clothes, put things away, etc. Nothing worked, so I made a chart. It was called, "What she'll be is up to me." I made little magnets called "Happy Mommy" and "Sad Mommy". "Happy Mommy" had an image of a happy mom and "Sad Mommy" had an image of a sad mom. They were a 1950's style woman—kind of quirky and fun. On the chart, I put John's name with a list of responsibilities and Jack's name with a list of responsibilities. I put days of the week across the top of the chart and hung it up in the dining room. They earned either "Happy Mommy" magnets or "Sad Mommy" magnets each day, depending upon if they completed their daily family responsibilities.

I never saw Jack so motivated to 'beat' his Dad. It really got both of their competitive juices going and served as a fun way to remind Jack of his family responsibilities.

Make sure you tell them how much their help around the house means to you; praise them often and sincerely. As they start their business, you will see them remember more often because the responsibility of the business will carry over and help them to remember their other responsibilities.

My preference is to use money incentives as a tool; show our kids they have earning potential. Pay them to do something out of the ordinary, like wash your car, clean the garage or help you plant the vegetable garden. These are jobs which show them they have earning power outside of everyday life. Make a list of these jobs with prices you will pay and post the list somewhere in the house. Jack knows—if he wants extra money—there is a standing offer to wash my car for $10. He knows he has earning potential. He can sell me a service. I am a willing customer. All he has to do is "Work It".

## *What is involved in running a business?*

> *"The child supplies the power but the parents have to do the steering."*
>
> —*Dr. Benjamin Spock, MD*

The act of helping your kid start a business will provide you with many teaching moments. During the course of starting the business—at the minimum—it will be your job to teach these five basic business concepts:

- Marketing and Sales
- Accounting
- Execution
- Customer Service
- Follow-up

Once they start their own business, kids are exposed to—and become more aware of—these concepts which before were merely a part of the outside world. "Marketing" suddenly becomes a word they will use when they observe other businesses. "Customer Service" at a store takes on a whole new meaning as you and your child interact with other business owners. There will be opportunities for discussions at a higher level than you ever realized.

From beginning to end, the process of starting and running the business will introduce, hone and reinforce the six millionaire skills you are teaching your kids. The examples and lessons will be real life and hands-on. The level of learning will be deeper and more profound than you thought possible.

With this dawn of awareness comes a new world of responsibilities on your part. Losing it at the store because the clerk does not provide good customer service will water down the teaching moment; so be on your best behavior. It is hard to discuss someone else's bad behavior if you are a horse's patootie yourself!

## Changing Your Kids' Conversations with Money

> *"By the time a man realizes that maybe his father was right, he usually has a son who thinks he's wrong."*
> —*Charles Wadsworth*

How millionaires look at money and their attitudes towards it is unique. They are not caught up in the dollars. They see money as a tool they can leverage to get from point A to point B in their master plan.

As your kid realizes they have the capability to earn and make money, they will need your guidance to make sure they adopt a healthy relationship with capital. One of the most profound things that happened with Jack was the change in his conversation with and around money. I was actually surprised the first time he told me he thought having money was a bad thing. Surprised is probably an understatement; I was astonished! I did not know where he had picked up that notion, and I did not think it was from either his dad or me. I know there are many influences out there, so he might have picked it up from a number of sources. Or, we could have unwittingly and subconsciously put that thought into his head. What I knew—in my gut—was I had to change his way of thinking and quick.

Jack and I talked about the *good* you can do when you have money. We talked about the difference money can make in peoples' lives, and how having money—in excess of what you need—means you can help others. We worked on changing his perception that having money is bad and started working on understanding all the positive aspects about money.

I have the distinct honor of knowing Loral Langemeier—one of today's most dynamic and pioneering financial strategists. An author and a leading motivational speaker, Loral has spurred thousands across the country from dazed apathy and fear of finance to millionaire status. She offers people the simple tools they need to launch innovative businesses that generate cash and build wealth. The first time I picked up one of her books was after I saw her speak at a conference. Her message was very clear. Anyone can be a success. You simply have to believe in yourself and go after your dream with conviction.

Recently, she wrote a blog called *Start with a Healthy Money Mindset* in which she talked about "creating conversations with money".

She is the master, and here is some of what she wrote:

### Assess Your Limiting Beliefs

Money is one of those things you probably have strong opinions about. You may be aware of these opinions, or not, but close analysis is a must. Analyze all of the things you believe about money and write them down.

For example, do you believe you have to work hard to ever get rich? Add to that list all of the things your friends, parents and relatives said about money when you were growing up. For example, did you hear your parents or grandparents say money is the root of all evil? (Don't analyze your thoughts just yet.) Simply write down what you believe and what you heard growing up.

Now, one "belief" at a time, take a look each of your negative thoughts about money. Do you really believe that? Why do you believe it? Why not? What experiences support or disprove that belief?

It may take you several days to work through this list of beliefs. That's okay. At the end of the list you will have a new belief system about money. Because chances are the things you thought you believed about money aren't really true. For instance, the biblical verse is actually the love of money is the root of all evil. Contrary to Gordon Gekko's Greed is Good speech that he gave to the Teldar Paper shareholders in the movie, greed is not good. But money IS good. Not only can it make your life easier, you can do a lot of good through philanthropy once you have more of it.

### Affirmations

In other words, positive statements. "Everything I touch turns to gold!" Use affirmations to eliminate any negative thoughts about money. Change your relationship to money. It can take time to change your conversation in your head because it comes from deep within your psyche—but get started in replacing your negative thoughts with positive ones immediately.

When you recognize a negative money thought, replace it with a positive one. Write down the positive one and repeat it several times a day. Becoming conscious of your thoughts about money is the first step. Changing them to positive thoughts is the powerful second step.

### Good Habits

Finally, embrace your affirmations and new beliefs to create good money habits. These don't have to be major life changes. Small changes can make a big difference. For example, start setting aside $25 each week in a savings account. This small step can reap large rewards. Start paying off your credit cards by adding a little more money to each payment. Again, a small step but one that can really make you feel positive about your money.

### Conversation

Whether the conversation you have about money is in your head or out loud, keep it positive. When you catch yourself being negative realize that those thoughts are nothing but false beliefs.

Money is a part of life. Changing the way you think about it can change your life. Take a look at your beliefs. Explore your thoughts. Carry on positive conversations with yourself and others. And embrace new habits that make a real difference.[14]

Working with your kids to create a healthy relationship with money often starts with us. It is not easy, but it is critical for you to drink from the cup before you give your kids a sip. This was something I had to do and I found it quite liberating.

---

14  Loral Langemeier, *Start with a Healthy Money Mindset,* (Stateline, NV: Live Out Loud, April 2011)

I looked at what I was doing in my own business and realized I needed help to take it to the next level. I got involved with a number of mentoring programs and motivational seminars. During this learning process, I found my calling—if you will—to write this book and share my experiences with other parents and caregivers.

I did not plan this path but, the more I looked into it, the more I realized it was my passion. Regardless of where you are financially, you can give your kids the gift of being free to believe they can do what they set their minds to do. You can allow them to believe wealth and prosperity—which come with success—are wonderful things.

## The Art of Persistence

> *"Never raise your hand to your kids. It leaves your groin unprotected."*
>
> —*Red Buttons*

Persistence is an important quality for life. It is clearly an important hallmark of the "Work It" millionaire skill. Starting his own business, Jack learned he had to stick with something if he wanted to get better and better at it. He had been in Little League since he was in kindergarten, so he knew about practicing and getting better at something physical; however, the skills required to create a successful business were entirely new to him. The required persistence was harder to understand.

The need for practicing things other than the physical or cerebral is a hard concept to get across. Memorizing a math fact or practicing to catch a fly ball is a different skill from learning how to ask people to buy your product or service. In order to convince them they need to part with their money; you must possess an internal dialog of self confidence and belief in your product or service. It is hard to convey this concept, and it takes perseverance to really bring the concept home. We have all heard the *fake it till you make it* saying. There is a ring of truth to that statement but we can't teach our kids to fake it. Instead we have to teach them to believe in themselves and their business; often before they even make their first sale. This is the point at which you have to become their biggest and most important cheerleader.

Persistence can be a double-edged sword; teaching our kids how to ask and the art of persistence also deserves its own warning. Once you teach your kid to be persistent in their business; you need to be prepared for them to use the same set of persistent muscles when they are asking for things from you! The truth is, as they get better at asking it is harder to say "No" because they are now able to think on their feet and come up with creative reasons why you should say "Yes".

Prepare yourself. Jack and I often laugh our heads off when he starts doing this. I look at him and can tell he is working his "asking magic" on me; he knows he is doing it too! Kids who have been taught how to ask and the art of persistence realize quickly; if they present their request from a different direction or come at it from a different angle, it might work. Persistence becomes a skill they learn to work to their advantage. When your kid does this, you will know the lessons are sinking in and persistence is a skill they are starting to master.

It would be impossible for me to explain everything Jack has learned while running his business and, truth be told, I am sure there are other things he has yet to learn. If you were on the fence about whether it is a good idea to make this effort, I hope this chapter has removed those doubts.

## Why the Hood?

The kind of business your kid starts is limited only by their imagination. I purposefully encourage Jack to start a business in our neighborhood. Some of you might be saying to yourself, "My son makes the coolest t-shirts. He can sell them on the Internet." Or maybe you are saying, "My daughter is a software genius who is great at building android apps. I want her to sell them on-line."

Internet-based businesses are wonderful and I would never discourage them, however, the personal interaction your child will have with a neighborhood-based business will teach them a whole host of skills they will miss if they start an Internet only business. I urge you to look in your own backyard for their core business and make the Internet ventures ancillary income. Your hood is teeming with ideas and possibilities. The benefits of learning in-person customer service and sales skills should be embraced and promoted.

There are so many resources out there to help empower our kids.

Over the years and while I was writing this book I run into some wonderful resources I wanted to share.

I hope this page is helpful to you and you find some ideas and resources to help you empower your kids!

The subject matter is very diverse, so no doubt you'll find something of interest.

**www.howtoraiseamillionaire.com/kidpower**

*Chapter 2*

# How We Did It

*I hear and I forget.*
*I see and I remember.*
*I do and I understand.*

—*Confucius*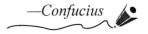

## *Encouraging Your Child to Start a Business*

For a long time, I had been thinking it would be fun for Jack to start a business. When he was about seven years old, I thought up the idea of "Jack's Garbage Valet" I thought at the time he was a little too young for the idea, but figured I would try it anyway.

Man, did I get an earful! Jack did not like the idea at all. Looking back, I see now he was not at a point in his young life where he could see the benefits of making money. It was just that simple. When we went to the store he did not ask for toys or beg me to buy him this or that, so I bided my time. I would occasionally suggest the idea and get the standard response.

"I don't want to do that, Mom."

Deep inside I knew Jack would benefit from starting a business, but to be honest, I had no real incentive to force the issue. It was not until after he had been bullied and his self-esteem was trashed that I made a concerted effort to woo him into action. The more I thought about it, the more I was convinced starting a business was one of the ways I could help him rebuild his self-esteem. But I still had Jack's reluctance to overcome.

As a parent sometimes we have to play one side of our kid's brain against the other. We have to exploit the desire they have for one thing to overcome objections of another. It might not be the nicest thing to admit, but hey, I am trying to be honest here. About the time Jack turned 10, he started to become aware of things he wanted to buy—things he *needed*. We would be in a store and he would say, "Mom, I *neeeeeeeed* this." It always made me laugh because it was always a *need*, not a *want*.

Don't you just love how kids *need* stuff? It is a testament to most of our upbringings that we have learned to say need, not want. How many of us have heard, "You don't want that…" from our parents. But kids, in genuine blissful naivety *need* stuff. We should all be so lucky to be back at the place where we *need* stuff. I digress.

I knew having him buy the stuff he *needed* with his own money was a good thing. I also knew I was setting him up! What I did not realize is I was setting him up for one of the greatest experiences he could have in life!

I will now reveal Jack's Achilles' heel: *Star Wars*—but not just any *Star Wars*—*Star Wars: The Clone Wars*. Yes, George Lucas, you have hooked another kid! Now, what does every good movie producer produce? *Action figures!* Yep, those lovely items with five hundred million little attachments, which inevitably are caught in the vacuum cleaner, eaten by the dog, stepped on in the middle of the night in your bare feet or lost in the black hole that is the Mom-mobile! Excuse me while I digress—again. Have you ever noticed how the most important part of the action figure always gets lost in the car while you are on the freeway or weaving through traffic? It is NEVER lost when you are driving up to the house or are parked in a parking lot. It is always a tragic moment just when you are in the thick of driving. Phew...had to get that out!

Let us take a moment and outline the rules for the art of collecting action figures:

- **Rule #1**: The action figure owner must buy the latest and greatest action figures; which come out almost *every other day*.
- **Rule #2**: The action figure owner must repurchase the action figures they already have if the dog has eaten them. In Jack's case, it was Captain Rex. The dogs chewed poor Captain Rex's helmet right off his little head. Everyone *knows* Captain Rex cannot function without his helmet—much less his head—which used to be attached under the helmet!

- **Rule #3**: Any lost action figure parts must be replaced at the owner's expense—if and only if—said action figure was strewn all over the owner's bedroom floor, left on the sofa, floating around the Mom-mobile, or abandoned in any location other than where it belonged; allowing the aforementioned dogs in Rule #2 access to eat them. Did

I fail to mention, pieces and parts of action figures are NOT sold separately. If you *need* to get a replacement helmet, gun or whatever, you have to buy a whole new action figure.

- **Rule #4**: If the dogs mutilate any part of a bad guy there is no written need to repurchase that action figure. (This is a Mom Rule.) This sucker is now *realistic* and the chewed-up arm is now a *war wound*—better yet, a *Star Wars War Wound*!

Jack came to appreciate Rule #4 and quickly adopted it because Rules #2 and #3 were bleeding him dry! Rule #4 meant half the population the dogs chewed did not have to be replaced! Now, if we could only teach dogs the difference between the good guys and the bad guys, we would be in business!

The beauty of Jack's obsession was he had something he *needed* to buy. We went to Target® one day—the one store that seems to carry the most of these little beauties—and I put out the snare. He found something he wanted, and I told him I could not keep buying these things for him. I told him he would have to use his own money. To his credit, he immediately agreed. When he got home, I made him pull the cash out of his bank. After a couple of trips to Target and as his funds dwindled—I knew I had him.

The next time he went to his bank to pull money out for an item, I suggested he needed to find a way to get money back *into* the bank. I brought up the Garbage Valet idea again. He balked.

No problem. I knew there would be a next time.

Then, the next time he had to go dip into the incredible shrinking piggy bank—to feed his obsession—he bit.

"Okay, Mom, I'll *do* it!"

## *Ready, Set, Market!*

With Jack's blessing, I flew into action. We created a flyer, printed out a boatload on the printer and we were ready to put the flyers around the neighborhood. It was summer and it just happened to be the day before garbage day. I would love to tell you I was clever enough to plan it all that way—that I had strategically taken him to the store on the day before garbage day, whet his appetite, set the snare and caught him—but it was just dumb luck. However, this much I knew—if I did not work quickly—I would lose him.

We grabbed a roll of packing tape, walked around the neighborhood and taped a flyer to every can at every house.

We practiced a sales pitch in case we ran into a neighbor:

> "Hi! My name is Jack James. I am your neighbor and I live on XYZ Street. Are you getting tired of taking your garbage cans in and out? Then hire me! For $10 a month, I'll take your cans in and out and you won't have to worry anymore."

It was simple, but he still had to practice. I knew from some of his Cub Scout activities he would get tongue-tied, so we went over his spiel several times. You know what? He *still* got tongue-tied! I helped nudge the conversation along by adding in the next word of his spiel when he got really stuck. I also took the opportunity to introduce myself to the neighbors by saying:

> "Hi! I'm Jack's Mom. If you decide you want Jack's service, just let us know."

I would remind Jack to hand them a flyer and we would go on to the next house. At a couple of houses, the neighbors were out front. He got to practice his spiel. If the cans were not out yet, he put the flyer on the porch; if the cans were out, he put the flyer on the can.

I do not know if your neighborhood is like ours but, sadly, we do not know many of our neighbors. When I was growing up, everyone knew everyone. As a kid, you could not get away with a thing because your parents always got a call from someone! It is not like that any longer. People keep more to themselves. I am sure it is because we are all so busy or because people are more cautious; but if you ask me, it's sad.

At about the 15th house, we ran into Janice, a delightful lady whom we met for the first time that day. She listened politely to Jack's spiel, which was still rough, and said, "Yes!"

*Holy cow!* She said, "Yes!" It is hard to describe what it was like to watch Jack get his first "Yes". He was so pleased and I was so proud. We continued to walk around the neighborhood and, at one point, we ran out of flyers. We zipped home and printed out more.

Something happened while we were putting out the flyers: *Jack was interested.* I did not expect him to show any interest because of my prior nagging; however, as soon as we got home to print more flyers, he quickly lost interest. It took some effort to get him back out and interested again. I could have saved myself a lot of effort.

The lesson here is to do a quick drive around the neighborhood and count the houses, so you will know how many flyers to print. We live in a hilly neighborhood so—for us—it was a double effort when we had to go home, go back out again and climb the hills twice.

With more flyers in hand, we continued our rounds and met with several neighbors. Jack gave his sales pitch (more about the sales pitch later in this chapter) and got better at it each time. It was actually fun! That day, he gave his sales pitch to about 15 neighbors.

As we were finishing, we ran into a neighbor, Lucia, about two doors up from us, whom we knew. Jack gave her the pitch and she signed up. Jack had *two* customers! It was an amazing day. Jack was thrilled and so was I.

Jack had a hard time understanding why more people did not sign up. He could not really understand why people were not jumping at the idea. If you have ever sold Girl Scout Cookies or anything else at a grocery store, you can understand how it takes a lot of *No's* to get a *Yes*. It is one thing to stand there and say, "would you like to buy X" person after person. It is a whole different ballgame to walk the streets, go to house after house and hear, "No thanks" time and time again. Just ask any seasoned sales person; this is not a game for wimps. For this very reason, this exercise is invaluable!

I explained to Jack most people had probably never thought about a service to have their cans taken in and out. With the flyer, we got the word out and we planned to put flyers out every so often. We did not want to be a nuisance to our neighbors, but we would remind them again the service was available. The more they heard about the service, the more they would think of engaging him. We'll talk later about how to teach fundamental sales and marketing skills – a valuable business skill.

The next week, Jack started his route.

I am not going to lie to you. Getting into the routine of taking the cans in and out was not easy. There were many days where we would take the cans out at 5 p.m. or later. Life gets in the way sometimes, and there were times when we had to make it work.

The best part has been Jack's customers. They are understanding and wonderful, and now we know more people in our neighborhood. When we put more flyers out, people say, "So *you're* the kid who does the cans! I have your flyer on my refrigerator." It is a great boost for Jack; I'll talk more about that in the next chapter.

About a month and a half later, we did another round of flyers. This time it was a smaller size flyer, (two per page) and we put them on the cans only. It was faster and cheaper, and I did not think a full-page flyer was necessary after the first time.

## Marketing at Every Opportunity

*"In marketing there are those who satisfy needs and those who create wants."*

—*Juan Carlos Castillo*

Our next step was to develop a brochure we could keep in the car while we were *out and about*. We thought of ancillary services (more business jargon Jack learned in the process of starting his business) he could offer besides the Garbage Valet. This brainstorming session helped Jack think of other things he could do around the neighborhood. We gave one to Lucia and she hired him to dog sit while she was on her business travels. She also hired him to pick all the lemons on her tree. It was something she needed done, he could do it, it was a perfect example of "find a need and fill it". It didn't cost her a fortune, she could mark something off her Ta-Da List and Jack made an extra

10 bucks! It was great! The brochure was working and it was a great tool. For those of you who think you just found a typo (Ta-Da List instead of To-Do List) you'll have to keep looking.☺ In our house, we don't have To-Do Lists; we have Ta-Da Lists. That way when we accomplish something or complete a task on our list, we can declare, "Ta-Da!" A To-Do List seems like work. On the other hand, our Ta-Da List celebrates our accomplishments and well, it is simply more fun!

December came around and we had our annual neighborhood Christmas Party, which had been going on for years, long before we had moved into the neighborhood. When we first moved into the neighborhood, hordes of people came to the party. Your house, and who originally owned it, identified you. We were not the James Family, but rather the James Family who lived in the Bauer's house. After 18 years and a lot of turnover in the neighborhood, the number of Christmas party attendees has gotten smaller and we are simply Jack and Ann on XYZ Street. The evening is delightful and a wonderful way to get to know people in the neighborhood.

I learned a valuable lesson at that party—a lesson I should have known but never thought of until it happened. We were at the party and Lucia started telling someone about Jack's business. I called him over and had him give his sales pitch. Lucia was great; I, however, forgot to bring flyers for this captive audience! They could have met Jack and he could have passed flyers out to everyone. It was a missed opportunity. I did have a few brochures in the car, so we ran out, got them and passed them around. That night, Jack picked up a new customer. Overall, we learned a valuable lesson: *Always be prepared.* It was time to make more flyers and brochures.

The night of the Christmas Party, Jack instituted a new policy: He gave Lucia a $5 Starbucks gift card for the referral she gave him. She had actually given him a number of referrals, but only one actually signed up. We added his referral policy to the brochure: "If you refer a neighbor and they start my service, I'll give you a $5 Starbucks gift card."

That new customer then referred Jack to two more customers, and so it has gone. We could be better and more aggressive about getting him new customers, but it is important to remember this is a marathon and not a sprint. I felt it was important to have a manageable number of customers. The more customers we had, the longer it took Jack to do the work. I wanted the amount of work to be manageable for someone of his age. Each year, as he matures and is able to handle more customers and the additional work we expand his business. This teaches another valuable business concept. Business growth is a critical factor in one's success. Grow too fast and you can lose control of the quality and product; grow too slow and you can miss opportunities for expansion. An important part of any business plan is growth. I was teaching Jack how to forecast and analyze the growth of his business. This is all part of the "Work It" millionaire skill; a successful mindset that creates an environment for growth and forward thinking.

## *Teaching Accounting*

> *For Daddy and Uncle John:*
> *An accountant is a well-balanced person!*
> *Old accountants never die, they just depreciate.*
> *Old accountants never die, they just lose their balance.*
> *Old accountants never die, they just lose their figures.*
> *—Unknown*

The next step in the business was to send out invoices. I wanted Jack to understand the basics of running a business, so we started by using Intuit QuickBooks®, which is an accounting software package for small business. I could have encouraged Jack to use Quicken®, or any other accounting software, to keep track in a notebook or on a spreadsheet; but I wanted to give Jack an advantage and a head start. Real companies have real accounting software, and QuickBooks is a great software tool which is easy to learn and use. It might not be what big companies use, but it is what many small businesses use. The very fact Jack was learning the concept of business accounting on business software was enough for me. QuickBooks happens to be the software I have used for more than 14 years running my own small business, so I was familiar with it and it was readily available to me.

Whether you use QuickBooks or some other method, it is important your child learn the basics of running a business. If you decide to use a spreadsheet or a notebook, our Fast Start Action Guide[15] also gives you the tools on paper (as well as electronic versions) you will need to make it happen. The method is not the key, learning the concepts and doing it is.

True confession time: Invoicing and collecting money are not my strong suits. As a matter of fact, of all the different aspects of this adventure, I struggle with the discipline of accounting the most. What do I mean? I procrastinate at doing this with Jack. Admittedly, it is a very bad habit. I am working on getting better and the system we devised to work around *my* bad habit has worked like a charm. The lesson here is to openly admit what you are not good at and find a solution.

At first, we invoiced at the end of each month; then, a few months would go by, and we would just not get it done. A few months turned into a few more months and—wow—were we behind. Some of Jack's clients were ahead of the game; one taped an envelope to their cans with Jack's fee at the end of each month. Another even came to our house and just plain gave Jack a check. Talk about one ashamed mom! I am lucky his customers have been so understanding.

It was really bothering me each time we went out, so I tried to think of an easier method. I thought about Mrs. Larson, the lady who taped the

15    Ann Morgan James, *How to Raise a Millionaire Fast Action Start Guide*, (San Jose, CA: HTRAM Press, January 2012)

money to her garbage cans. We decided to follow her lead and gave out 12 envelopes, one for each month of the year, so the clients could tape the envelope (money) onto the can at the end of every month. This method meant Jack didn't have to wait for me to help him with invoicing. Instead, Jack did his accounts receivable when he collected the cash; which worked out much better.

Jack's customers are the best—bar none! They have been understanding, patient and kind to Jack. However, this process has not been without its glitches. His business has not run like a well-oiled machine every week and we have had our moments. It will likely be the same for you, but it has been a wonderful journey for Jack and me.

We have talked about sales, marketing, and accounting; we have shared the details of Jack's referral policy and given examples of how it has gotten him more business. However, we have not yet talked about delivery of the service; which is where the rubber meets the road. We now call Jack's service to his customers his *route*—kind of like my brother's paper route when he was young.

## Service Delivery and Execution

> *God wisely designed the human body so that we can neither pat our own backs nor kick ourselves too easily.*
>
> *—Author Unknown*

Remember we started Jack's business in the summer, so walking around the neighborhood worked perfectly. There was no school at the time; therefore we were able to put the cans out at any time the day before pickup. This was both a good and a bad thing. We did not develop a real schedule during those summer months and we should have.

Actually, I do think the perfect time to start a business is in the summer. Because there is no school, you have the opportunity to get into a good routine. If you are smart—which we were not—keep the school schedule in mind and go out as if school were in session to give yourselves practice. When school started, we had to readjust to our school schedule, which was something we could have avoided. With this book, you will learn from my mistakes and you can use my roadmap to prevent pitfalls of your own.

At first, we walked around the neighborhood; it was great exercise and we both enjoyed doing it. At least that was the pipedream I kept handing myself. The truth is, at times, it was a chore; but after a few months of being paid, the chore part faded and it became a means to an end.

Jack took the job very seriously and was extremely conscientious. He made sure he put the cans out just so—not too closely together, not in the gutter, not in the driveway or by the mailbox. Honestly, I had not seen him that meticulous before. Sure, he was thoughtful about some things, but nothing like this. I was pleased and surprised. He really took his business to heart. Bingo! We were well on our way to cultivating the "Love It" and "Work It" millionaire skills.

As Jack got new customers, and when school started, we simply didn't have as much free time. Between school, homework, music lessons and other outside interests we had to be more mindful of our time, so we started driving around the neighborhood to do his route. With homework and other commitments, efficiency became more critical. As summer approached once more, we started to walk again, but to be honest, whatever the season, we mostly drove.

## Teaching How to Ask

> *Sing like no one's listening, love like you've never been hurt, dance like nobody's watching. and live like it's heaven on earth.*
>
> —*Mark Twain*

How many of you get notices of fundraisers from your kid's school, youth or sports groups, and take them to work so you can sell the swag there? Maybe you buy a bunch of stuff—as I do—to avoid taking the fundraiser notice to work. If you use this and other tricks to get out of helping your kid sell these things, you are not alone. If you actually take your kid and sell them door-to-door, you are a very rare breed!

Most of us take the catalog or candy to work, put them on our desk, and sell them to all the other parents who have sold us stuff for their kids. Kids rarely do the selling anymore. I know it is a pain in the rear to take them around the neighborhood but, if you do not, they are missing an opportunity to learn how to talk to adults and strangers. No doubt you have already read a little about this subject in Chapter 1, under the section entitled: *Teaching How to Talk to Adults*. No, you are not dreaming, I *am* repeating myself. Statistics say you have to hear or read something three times to retain it. I feel so passionately about this subject, I think it bears repeating.

Taking your kid around the neighborhood leads to three positive lessons:

1. It gives them practice talking to strangers
2. It boosts their self-esteem
3. It teaches them how to ask

All three lessons are essential key elements to the millionaire mindset. Successful businesspeople have a high level of self-esteem, which enables them to talk to people whom they have never met. It takes self-confidence to put oneself out there. It takes self-confidence to pitch a stranger a business idea.

This skill reinforces and strengthens a number of my millionaire skills including, "Believe It", "Love It" and "Work It". You'll find as you read this book and begin to put these principles into action, many of the skills and much of the learning overlaps. That is not by accident. They are all interrelated and once you see them in action, you will discover additional lessons I have not articulated. That is half the fun! Teaching moments will crop up in the most unlikely places and because you are aware you are teaching, you'll learn to recognize and take advantage of every opportunity.

What I am suggesting is not an easy task; I'll grant you it takes time and effort. I know your pain. I do not work in a traditional office, so I don't have an office to take the stuff to anyway. Much of my family is not physically close to us, so it is hard to hit Uncle Buck up for a bunch of cash. We do a lot of door-to-door selling with Jack's business, and we approach the neighbors with some of the charitable activities we do as well.

That said, every chance I get to have Jack out selling something, I take it! For example, because we are in scouting, fundraisers come with the territory. Every time there is an opportunity Jack works the "Show and Sell" and stands outside a store hawking scouting stuff. There are times when our schedule won't allow Jack to participate. One year, the woman organizing the fundraising activities for Jack's troop, Mrs. McDonald Nelson, decided to have the scouts sell popcorn outside our local banks on payday—*brilliant!* Like clockwork, a host of people go to the bank on payday, cash their checks and come out of the bank with money. Go to your bank and ask the manger if your kid can sell their fundraiser items in front of the bank on the first or third Friday. Take a card table, have your child dress in their school uniform or field trip tee shirt and help them sell for two hours between 4 and 6 p.m. You will be amazed how much they will sell!

## Popsicle® Prose

It is one thing to help you kid with goal setting and being positive, but let's face it, we are not with them all day long. There are going to be times when they need a boost; a reminder of what they are going after or how unbelievably special they are. I came up with this idea by accident. Jack and I were listening to Jack Canfield one morning in the car on the way to school. He was teaching his listeners to write down their affirmations on a card or piece of paper and take it out and read it a couple of times during the day. I really wanted Jack to be able to think good thoughts during school but I didn't have any paper. I looked down and saw a bunch of big tongue depressors—you know, giant Popsicle sticks. I had recently taught a class of scout leaders how to safely teach kids to use pocket knives and I used big tongue depressors in my class. I had a bunch still in the car. I grabbed a stick and a sharpie and wrote down our affirmations; one popsicle stick for Jack and one popsicle stick for me. We put them in our pockets and were on our way!

They worked like a charm. I now keep a supply of popsicle sticks in my car and we use them often! They are a great way to start the day off in a positive light and keep that positive light glowing all day long.

This will be an opportunity to teach your kid another sales pitch—one for the thing they are selling—which is great practice. This experience will give them the chance to talk to strangers and practice taking rejections (read "No") gracefully. Have your kid open the door and say, "Have a nice day!" Remember: There are 20 potential customers who will say "No" on the road to one "Yes". Make it a game and have fun. Practice asking. Practice talking to strangers. Practice skills they can use for life. Take every opportunity you can find to work on the "Love It" and "Work It" millionaire skills! This is a great chance for both. If they ask with enthusiasm they will get a better response. Remember the Markita Andrews story from Chapter 1, she got her prospects invested in her goals. She drew them into her dream and because they were helping her reach a goal, they were more invested in the purchase. Teaching good eye contact and proper manners—all the while—you are teaching them how to be resilient.

In Chapter 1, we talked about the art of asking, and The 8 Principles of Asking—The Aladdin Factor—as taught by Jack Canfield and Mark Victor Hansen.[16] Again, this is perfect reinforcement of the "Believe It", "Love It" and "Work It" millionaire skills.

Here is how Jack has used the principles in his Garbage Valet business:

1. **Ask as if you expect to get it.**

   When Jack started asking his neighbors for business, it was clear he did not believe in what he was saying. This lack of confidence went right to the heart of this first principle. Confidence in himself and his product was something that had to build inside of Jack, and it took time. At first he didn't ask as if he expected to get it. This is where my encouragement—and, yes, sometimes nagging—helped him remain buoyed at times when he wanted to just plain quit. Once his confidence grew, I encouraged asking as if it were expected. This is hard for a young person to grasp, but they catch on. When they do catch on, you can see the light in their eyes and it is beyond encouraging. These are the moments—the victories—that make all the effort worthwhile. It also teaches them how to accept "No" gracefully. Learning "No" is part of the sales process and not a personal rebuff helps to increase their self-esteem and helps them learn to handle rejection. Let's be honest, there are plenty of times I take things way too personally. It often takes someone looking at a situation from the outside to tell me I am off base. Sometimes I need someone I trust to tell me I am being too sensitive. This is often an unwelcome message, but true just the same. If we are able to teach our kids to look more objectively at a

---

16 Jack Canfield and Mark Victor Hansen, *The Aladdin Factor: Anything is possible - If you dare to ask!* (New York, NY, Macmillan Audio, 1995)

negative response, we will help them develop a healthier overall sense of self-esteem. You are helping set them up for life!

2. **Ask with conviction.**

This principle is very similar to Principle #1 (Ask as if you expect to get it) and it's difficult to teach kids to understand the difference. I was teaching Jack to be a little more sincere when he pitched his services as opposed to having conviction, but we are ultimately talking about believing in what you are selling. Back to that "Believe It" millionaire skill. When you believe in something you exude natural enthusiasm. It is genuine and people can see and feel the belief you have in yourself and your product. This is where you ultimately want to get them. Understand, once they have their first sale and they are performing their service or delivering their product, believing in the business is easier. Once the sense of belief is established and they start seeing the fruits of their labors, they will be in a place where they can begin to "Love It".

3. **Ask someone who can give it to you.**

This principle is common sense, but it might not be obvious. I don't know about you, but there have been plenty of times I have called a customer service line, told the person answering the phone the whole story behind my call, only to have that person tell me I needed to talk to his or her supervisor. This is a lesson in time management—one I am still learning—one I hope to help teach Jack early. As we went around the neighborhood, I tried to teach Jack how to ask the right questions so he did not give his sales pitch to people who were not the decision makers. In other words, do not ask the kid who lives at the house if you can mow their lawn every week; they will have to ask their parents. Instead, find out if the parents are at home and ask them!

4. **Be clear and specific.**

I helped Jack make sure his message was very clear about what he would do and how much it would cost. This is very important and easy for them to understand. Talking it out with them really helps them get a clear picture of how to do it and why it is important. Try role playing—you be a neighbor. Have your child approach you— from beginning to end—Introduction, Sales Pitch and Close. The more practice they get, the better they are at it. Practice, practice, practice.

5. **Ask from your heart.**

Being genuine is such an important part of life in general. It is simple and pure. Teach them to be real, teach them to mean what they say and only say what they mean. If you are genuine with your approach to helping them start their business, they will pick up their cues from you. When I started this process, I was teaching from my heart and he grasped it quickly. Your kid will too!

6. **Ask with humor and creativity.**

This principle is so perfect for a kid and it came naturally to Jack. Help your kids learn that humor is a wonderful tool and used correctly it can make people feel good. Any time we encourage creativity in our kids and help their imaginations soar is a time we help boost their self-worth. We found humor was easy to use with the flyers. One of Jack's flyers says, "Ever panic because you forgot to put the cans out and you can hear the truck rumble by?" Another says, "Aren't you tired of dragging me to the curb and back. Hire Jack!" They are all fun ways to deliver his message. When he sees a neighbor pull their cans out, he will say, "Hey! Hire me. I can do that for you!" and gives them a brochure.

We always try to think of fun ways to sell his product. (Imagine what someone could do if they had a pooper-scooper business!) I was in the parking lot of my local grocery store the other day and saw one of those cars, all wrapped, advertising their business. Guess what their business was—*pooper-scooper*! It was funny and tastefully done. You can bet that car brings them a lot of new customers.

7. **Give in order to get.**

This is a great principle because it teaches your kids to give first before they expect anything. Often, when Jack has a prospect, especially when he has someone who seems to be on the fence about his service, he offers to do their cans free for one month. The first time I suggested this, I saw in his eyes he thought I had lost my mind. However reluctant he was, he offered the free month of service just the same. After he did her cans for a month, he went back to Miss Maxine's house and said, "Miss Maxine would you like me to continue the service?" and she said, "Yes!" I knew he got the picture. This was also the principle behind the Starbucks referral gift cards. Thanking his customers is very important and a good way for him to see results. It teaches our kids to come from a place of service. It is part and parcel to my "Give It" millionaire skill. When we give—when we come from a place of service—we get so much more in return.

This asking principle also works on the "Believe It" millionaire skill. To be able to give your product or service away, you have to believe in it. You have to believe your service or product is so good that when they try it, they will want more.

8. **Ask repeatedly.**

This asking principle goes back to the notion of asking 20 times to get one "Yes". We have got to teach our kids to *ask, ask, ask!* It teaches them self-esteem, tenacity, and character! These skills will definitely be required in the future. If they decide to work for someone else they will have to go job hunting. They will have to be able to knock on doors, ask for the job and move on to the next prospect when they get a rejection. This is the perfect opportunity to build character in minds that absorb like a sponge. This is why your job of head cheerleader is so important! You'll need to be the one to keep them positive. You will need to be the one that says "Next". At first, they won't like the rejection. Our society continually tries to build a world for our kids where they can't fail. Everyone gets on the team; everyone hits; everyone does a great job; everyone is the best. What we end up with is a growing number of children who never learned how to handle rejection. Teaching kids how to ask does not create the expectation of entitlement. It is a skill we all can learn and is not for the faint of heart. It is important. It is realistic. In life, we often have to ask multiple times before receiving. When you ask a prospect for a sale, you can't pitch a fit if they say "No". This in itself is an important lesson. I have noticed now when my response is "No", Jack's wheels are turning and he is already hard at working thinking of other ways to ask or get what he is looking for—necessity has become the mother of invention and Jack has learned how to invent new ways to ask for the same thing.

## The Fast Start Action Guide

*The best inheritance a parent can give his children is
a few minutes of his time each day.*
> —Orlando A. Battista

Remember before we ever started this process, I had the business idea, service and name, years in advance. I had also been working on him for a while. If you are just getting started on a business idea for your kid, you will have to add a few steps to the process.

Our Fast Start Action Guide pulls together all the things any parent would need to help their kid start their own business. Whenever possible, I believe one should avoid reinventing the wheel, so our action guide offers all the needed materials to start a business in five days. The Fast Start Action Guide comes in an electronic format for quick and easy download. For those who want it in paper form, the guide is also available in print. Either version can be ordered from our website howtoraiseamillionaire.com. Click on our product page and look under the Implementation section. We also offer Action Guides for all six millionaire skills. These Action Guides give you additional activities you can do with your kids to help them learn and practice to "Dream It", "Believe It", "Love It", "Work It", "Own It" and "Give It".

Teaching kids how to set goals and go after those goals is such an important skill, I wanted to devote an entire page to it.

On this page you'll find a number of different books and resources to help you teach your kids the important skill of goal setting. Remember, like I said, we all have more than one cookbook. If you get one nugget out of these, it will be worth the investment!

**www.howtoraiseamillionaire.com/goalsetting**

*Chapter 3:*

# The Results

*"In the final analysis it is not what you do for your children but what you have taught them to do for themselves that will make them successful human beings."*

—*Ann Landers*

## *My Passion, Lessons, and Goals*

To be honest, I did not start out thinking of all the things Jack would learn from starting his own business. I did not encourage him to start his business because somebody told me it would be great and I should do this for him. I did it because I knew Jack needed a boost. His self-esteem had taken such a hit from the bullying and the Dyslexia that he was really in a very low place. He had no self-confidence. He considered everything he did to be "stupid". That was his word and it broke my heart every time I heard him say it.

All I knew was I had to do something to get him a win. I had to do something to boost his self-worth. I had to do something to give him back his confidence. What I realized was I was teaching him the things my parents had taught me. My folks died long before Jack started school and the downward spiral to where he was now. Inadvertently, I went back to my roots. I started teaching Jack the skills my parents had taught my brother and me. It was more dumb luck than anything else.

Deep down, I knew there would be positive principles in it for him to learn, but I did not see all the hidden benefits—or identify them as millionaire skills—that is until I was right in the middle of them and they revealed themselves to me over time. Seeing Jack mature before my eyes inspired this book. I wrote it so others could learn the benefits of making this extra effort with their children. Plenty of people will find excuse after excuse not to make the effort, but for those of you who push through those excuses and make it happen, you will be astounded!

Chapter 1 discusses some of the ideas I offer in this chapter, so it may seem redundant; for this, I do *not* apologize. We all need to hear things more than once for them to sink in.

There are differences in the way millionaires think. There are differences in the ways they approach life. I was lucky my parents taught me; I do not know if they realized what they were doing at the time, but the lessons were there nonetheless.

My goal is to start the dialog among parents, talk about these millionaire skills and knowingly and intentionally teach them—*on purpose*—with no apologies or hesitations. I want my kid to have every possible advantage in this world, and I am not ashamed to say I am teaching him millionaire skills. I know you won't be either.

In teaching these six principles—these skills—I came across other lessons, which your kids will learn as you help them start their own business. I have touched on these specific lessons and categorized them under one of my six millionaire skills because I was excited about Jack learning these lessons.

I wanted to make sure, when you start down the path with your children, you notice when these teaching moments arise—because they will! Most kids will not learn these skills unless you make the effort to teach them. You have to be aware. Once you activate—for lack of a better word—or tune in your mind to these skills; you'll see them crop up in additional opportunities—ones I have not enumerated. I would love to hear your experiences and have you share them with other parents. We are in this together. Go to our website howtoraiseamillionaire.com and share your experiences—the good, the bad and the gotchas!

## *Millionaire Skill #1: Dream It*

The first thing our kids need to learn is how to dream. Millionaires are able to see things in the aggregate. That is to say, they dream a dream and see the end game; they see the whole dream. As an example, Roger Bannister—the athlete who broke the four-minute mile—was an Olympian in the 1952 games.

He ran the 1500 meter final race but finished fourth, out of medal contention.

At that disappointing moment, Sir Bannister says he consciously set the goal of breaking the four-minute mile and—in fact—he envisioned *every* step of the race. Up until that time, no one had run a mile in under four minutes. He saw the dream in his mind's eye. On May 6, 1954, Bannister achieved his goal. His time for the mile was 3 minutes 59.4 seconds.

Since that historic day, many people have broken his record, but Sir Roger Bannister was the first to dream it and make it happen. I like the Bannister story because it powerfully illustrates something we can all understand. We have all run a race, whether in fun on the playground or in earnest on the track field. In his day, everyone considered Bannister's accomplishment impossible, but he dreamed it *was* possible and set out to make his specific and tangible dream come true. This example illustrates we should dream and, when we do, dream *specifically*.

Most kids have probably never thought of starting their own business. Is it because Mom and Dad do not own a business? Maybe. Is it because kids do not think the work they do has the potential of being a viable and honest-to-goodness business? Again—maybe. I think it is much more simple than any of those reasons. I think it is because we—their parents—do not present them with the opportunity.

Let's be honest: money makes our world thrive. As our current recession illustrates, the power of money is never more evident than when money is tight. It might not be something you like to think about, but money is powerful. I want my son to know he can harness the power of money any time he wants. *It is just that simple.*

One day, while driving home from school, Jack suddenly burst into tears. When I asked him why he was crying, his answer stopped me dead in my tracks.

"I am afraid that, when I grow up, there won't be any jobs and I won't be able to make a living for my family."

My 10-year-old was crying because he was worried about the economy. I could not believe it! What on earth made him think about that? Then I started to realize he hears all the scary stuff on the news, at school, in the grocery store, and all over the place. I paused to think about my answer.

"The economy is struggling, isn't it, Jack? You have heard about how people are having a hard time, haven't you? Even so, people are still driving, buying gas, shopping at stores, going about their lives and spending money, aren't they? They still have money to spend, don't they? So what does a smart businessperson do?"

He thought about it and I let him answer.

"They sell things people want to buy?"

"That's right!" I said. "Think about your business. Despite the fact people are having a hard time making money; they still buy your services, don't they? You have found something some people want. Does everyone in the neighborhood buy your service?"

"No," he answered, "but some do."

"That's right. So, if people stop buying your services, what would you do?"

"I would find something else they want to buy."

"Exactly! Jack, you are learning you can start a business doing anything, anytime, anywhere, as long as you think of something people need or want. You never have to worry about what the economy is like as long as you have the skills to figure out what business will work."

It was very deep stuff and I was amazed at our exchange of ideas. I won't tell you it put all of Jack's fears to rest, but he did start to think about his business and the things he was learning in a different and profound way.

He was learning—if he can dream it—he can create it.

As a rule, we don't watch violence on TV and we don't dwell on negative news. But both happen in our world. I think it is important to strike a balance. I was not naïve. I knew where Jack had heard the things about the economy. I am pleased he knew he could come to me with questions. I was pleased he knew he could have grown-up conversations with me as his Trusted Advisor. Again I was laying the groundwork for a very important concept I knew would come in handy when he really hits his teenage years. More on Trusted Advisor later!

## Goal Setting is the First Step to Dreaming It

> *"If you raise your children to feel that they can accomplish any goal or task they decide upon, you will have succeeded as a parent and you will have given your children the greatest of all blessings."*
>
> —*Brian Tracy*

For years there has been an urban myth about a study done by a top Ivy League university. The study says only 3% of people take the time to write down their goals. Lots of motivational consultants and speakers have cited this study for years and while it is pure conjecture, I would be willing to guess, the 3% cited in the mythical study is not far off from the truth.

Whether or not it is 3%, 13% or 30%, there was an important point those who cited the study were trying to get across. Write down your goals, put a plan into place, take action on the plan, and you'll have a greater chance of achieving your goals. Oh by the way—thanks to one very cool professor over at Dominican University—there is a new study to support the hypothesis![17]

Dr. Matthews was just like the rest of us, she had heard about the studies about goal setting. Sometimes the story was Harvard and sometimes Yale, but after much research, she, Steven Kraus (a social psychologist from Harvard), and investigative reporters at Fast Company figured out it was all an urban legend. There was never any study done!

That is where Dr. Matthews rides in! She decided to do a study of her own and it is great stuff. In a nutshell, her research backs up the assertions from the tall tale—the much-touted Yale/Harvard study.

Matthews found that when people wrote down their goals, shared them with a friend and sent weekly updates to that friend, on average, they were 33% more successful in accomplishing their stated goals than those who merely thought about their goals.

"My study provides empirical evidence for the effectiveness of three coaching tools: accountability, commitment, and writing down one's goals," Matthews said.

Here is what happened in Dr. Matthews' study. In the end, the individuals who were asked to simply think about the goals they hoped to accomplish only accomplished 43% of their stated goals. Those who had to write goals, write action commitments and also share those commitments with a friend accomplished 64% of their stated goals. Those who had to write goals, write action commitments, share their commitments with a friend and had to send a weekly progress report to their friend were the most successful. They were able to accomplish an average 76% of their goals.

---

17 Dr. Gail Matthews, Ph.D., *Goals Research,* Dr. Gail Matthews, Ph.D., (Dominican University, 2007)

The fact is, many motivational speakers and success gurus (such as Brian Tracy, Jack Canfield, Mark Victor Hansen, and Tony Robbins) tell us if you write down your top 10 goals, select the one you think will have the biggest impact in your life and try to accomplish it, you will be amazed at how your life is affected. You know what, they are right and now it turns out we have data to prove it. This study was done over a 4 week period. You have got to figure the people who were part of this study and were asked to work on their goals were highly motivated to get them done. Imagine what the statistics would have been if the study was done over a longer period of time. I would venture to guess a lot of those who just thought of their goals would never get them done. My guess is—in the end—the 3% from the urban myth would not be too far off.

Goal setting should be part of starting a business. To be honest, I have never been a goal setter. My parents taught me to have goals but they didn't teach me to write them down. As part of this journey, Jack and I have written down our goals and hung them on our hallway wall. We wrote each of our goals on a huge piece of butcher paper, and we pass by them every day and work toward them.

Life has thrown us some unexpected curves, and goal setting has made a profound difference in keeping our lives

*See our Goal Sheets!*

moving forward in a positive and uplifting way. This is what millionaires do: They dream, set goals and make action lists to achieve their goals. They make themselves accountable and they take action!

I did not think Jack's business would have led me to start goal setting, but I can tell you I am glad it did. Jack has changed so much since he has had goals. They have become something that drives him to take action all on his own. Honestly, I didn't expect it to mean much to me, but it has. I am amazed at what goal setting has done in my own life. I urge you to teach your child to write down their dreams and turn them into goals. While they are writing their goals, write your own. This is one of the first exercises in our Fast Start Action Guide.

When we help our kids dream big, they achieve big. I told you I learned a lot through this process. It is never too late to "Dream It"—even for an old mom like me!

## *Millionaire Skill #2: Believe It*

> *"I'm not old enough to play baseball or football. I'm not eight yet. My mom told me when you start baseball, you aren't going to be able to run that fast because you had an operation. I told Mom I wouldn't need to run that fast. When I play baseball, I'll just hit them out of the park. Then I'll be able to walk."*
> —*Edward J. McGrath, Jr.*

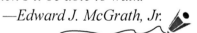

Once our kids learn to "Dream It", they need to believe their dreams are possible. This is an important skill; learning and practicing how *not to let* the noise get to you. It is a sad—but true—fact of life; there will be people in our kids' lives who will not believe in their dreams and cannot see them achieving their vision. These people will think of our kids' dreams as—just wishful thinking—not a goal. Our kids need to know this sad fact of life. Often times these people are not doing it out of spite or malice; sometimes they are doing it because they *care and worry* about us. Perhaps they can't see the vision; perhaps they want to make sure we don't get hurt; some might even be jealous. It is not worth the effort to figure out their motives. We simply need to learn how to turn off the noise and negative chatter; whether it comes from an outside source or ourselves. Believing our dreams are possible is not always easy.

Once you let yourself go, dreaming it is easy, but believing it is another story. Jack and I seek help from outside experts in order to bolster our "Believe It" millionaire skill.

Jack Canfield and Les Brown are two of my favorite motivational speakers. Mr. Canfield has a number of wonderful products, but one of the very best is from his Dream Big collection. I bought the collections for both Jack and me. It is called the *Vision Board Collection*. The program for kids and teens is called the "Teen Dream Big Collection[18]," and it includes the following:

- Teen Dream Big™ Vision Book
- Teen Vision Book Accessories
- The Key to Living the Law of Attraction
- Gratitude: A Daily Journal

Almost every day on the way to school, Jack and I listen to *The Key to Living the Law of Attraction* on CD—included in the collection. Each segment takes about five minutes. The CD teaches a number of the Law of Attraction principles. I think my favorite, and one which has been very powerful for both Jack and me, is the use of affirmations. After we started listening to the CD, I started keeping a supply of tongue depressors and a Sharpie® in my car. (Paper would work just fine.) At the end of each session, we each write down a positive affirmation on a stick. Jack carries his stick in his backpack; I keep mine in my pocket.

The idea is to take out that day's affirmation a couple of times during the day and tell ourselves our goal or affirmation.

Jack and I are thrilled to offer our own *How to Raise a Millionaire Vision Books[19]*. It was specially made for us by Ms. Watkins, the creator of the vision books in Jack Canfield's *Dream Big Collection*. I encourage you to use

*See Ann and Jack's Vision Books*

18  D.D. Watkins, *The Dream Big® Vision Book*, (Santa Barbara, CA: D.D. Watkins, 2008)
19  Ann Morgan James, *How to Raise a Millionaire Vision Book*, (San Jose, CA: HTRAM Press, January 2012)

our How to Raise a Millionaire Vision Books to enable your kids to visualize their dreams every day, with pictures, quotes and power words. I did my own vision book with Jack. I wanted him to know it was something I took seriously. I love my vision book! We keep both of our vision books in our bedrooms, so we can see them often!

Starting your day with your visions in mind gives you purpose and direction. We offer both a teen vision book and an adult vision book. We also offer them in a package along with our Thankful Thoughts Journal and some other inspirational tools. Like our other support materials, they can be found at howtoraiseamillionaire.com.

If you invest time to build your child a host of inspirational tools; the process of visualization will become a habit and part of their daily routine. It is a powerful way to reinforce the "Dream It", "Believe It" and "Love It" millionaire skills.

Jack and I also strive each day to write a few sentences about what we are grateful for, in our *Thankful Thoughts* journal. Jack's are often the same each day, but the important part is, he starts each day from a thankful place. As he matures, his dreams and goals will change and mature with him; so will what he is grateful for. Right now, we are creating a habit—a good one at that! We make a conscious effort to say aloud we are thankful for the gifts in our lives, for each other, for what we have and who we are.

Our Vision Books and butcher paper goals help us to keep our eyes on the prize. They give us a visual, fun way to select and then see our goals. They help to keep our goals clear in our minds and get us closer to the place we want to be.

We also put our affirmations, positive thoughts about ourselves and what we want to be on 3x5 cards and put them on our bathroom mirrors. The goal is to say them out loud to ourselves every day. Post-it Notes® work great too and they come in vibrant colors. What a great way to start the day!

These tools also helped me change my role from lecturer to helper. Because I am doing it too, this "lead by example" stance helps put me in that Trusted Advisor role.

Because I do them too, it helps Jack to see these things are *not* just for him because it is some kind of learning thing. He sees it is something I do as well. I want him to see we are never too old to learn and grow. If I do these things myself, they must be good things, he can trust me to give him advice I take myself. So often, I heard myself tell Jack it was my job to help him achieve his goals in life. You know you are in trouble when your 10-year-old tells you, "Stop lecturing me, Mom!"

Once Jack set his own goals, we both knew where he wanted to go. It also helped him see my requests of him were not for my benefit but were to help him reach the goals he had set for himself.

Here is an example: one of Jack's goals is to get rid of the dark circles under his eyes. I do not see them often, but he does occasionally get dark circles. We all know what those come from, not enough sleep. The other night, he balked about going to bed. Previously, it had taken at least half an hour from the time I uttered the phrase, "time for bed", to the time he was actually *in* bed.

Now, I no longer fight with Jack about bedtime. I simply say (in a very nice and sympathetic tone), "You said you wanted to get rid of those dark circles, didn't you? You know not getting enough sleep at night is one of the major causes of dark circles, don't you? I am not trying to make you go to bed early; I am just trying to help you achieve one of your goals. If you stay up and read your new magazine, you won't get as much sleep as you need, will you? It would be a better idea to go to bed now and read the book tomorrow when you get home from school wouldn't it?"

It is amazing. Ending questions with "wouldn't you?", "don't you?" and "didn't you?" eliminates the need to lecture.

I am sincere—not condescending or manipulative—when I ask the questions, because what I am saying is true. I ask the questions and he truthfully answers "Yes" to each one. It becomes *his* idea to go to bed so he can work towards *his* goal.

If what I am asking for helps get him closer to one of his goals, then he has bought into the request. I am learning to leverage his goals and approach him more from a place of service rather than as a dictator. As Jack gets older, *I* am learning to transition how *I* approach him in a way appropriate for his age. *I* am learning *how* to be a Trusted Advisor. Don't you just love it?

## Bye-Bye, Bad Dreams

My dear friend, Gail, taught this to me, and it works like a charm!

If you have a kid who has bad dreams, try this trick. Important Note: You have to do this with absolute seriousness.

When your child cries out in the night because they are having a bad dream, go into their room, ask them what the problem is. When you are told it is a bad dream, look past them at the pillow, be very surprised, and say—very matter-of-factly—"Well, no wonder you were having a bad dream! You have the bad dream side of the pillow up!"

Take the pillow out and ceremoniously turn it over, declaring now the "good dream" side of the pillow is up and their bad dreams will be all gone.

Fluff the pillow and smooth it out with great fanfare, all the while being very serious about what you just said. You can't laugh or make any kind of gesture that would make them think you are anything but the most serious of serious!

Thanks Gail.

You do not have to start this way or spend a bunch of money; a poster board will work fine as a vision board. There are plenty of books and motivational materials on-line or at the library. The point is to start kids early setting goals and creating mental mindsets so they can dream, believe in those dreams, and go after them. Helping them visually see their dream is important. It helps the mind see the dream as real.

You might be saying, "Why is she talking about this stuff? I thought this was a book about helping kids start a business?"

It is, but building self-esteem is part of the process. Our goal is to set up our kids with the tools they need to succeed. We want to give them every advantage to become all they want to be. I don't know about you, I don't care if the Harvard/Yale urban legend is bogus, I am going with it. If 3% of people set goals, you can bet that 3% includes all the Donald Trumps, Bill Gates, and Warren Buffets of the world. I am going to teach these life skills to my kid! This is the *millionaire* part of the package; it is one way millionaires think and act differently from most people. I want my son—and me for that matter—to try it.

What is stopping you?

## *Self-esteem and Confidence is Believing in Yourself*

> *"Promise me you will always remember – You are braver than you believe, stronger than you seem and smarter than you think"*
> —*Christopher Robin to Pooh*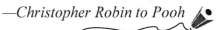

When we first went out into our neighborhood to sell Jack's business, I was a bit surprised. He has always been an outspoken kid, and rarely have I seen him afraid to speak to people or shy away from anyone.

As we walked around the neighborhood, he practiced his sales pitch and we saw our first victim. I thought Jack would march right up to this person and pitch, but I noticed he was reluctant and did not have much confidence in what he was saying.

The light went on! We have all met a salesperson who does not give us a very good sales pitch. When it is weak and half-hearted, you almost feel sorry for them; you may want to buy something just because you see them struggling with the words. Seeing Jack, I was brought back to my own Girl Scout days when I went door to door with my friend Mary selling calendars. I would go to a door, ring the bell and say, "Hi, my name is Ann, I am your neighbor, you don't want to buy a Girl Scout Calendar do you?" It was torture. Truth was, I thought the calendars were lame and I am sure the prospective customers could tell.

Now, as an adult, I hear this all the time with telemarketers who call the house. I imagine some person on the other end of the phone, sitting there cringing, barely making it through their required speech; often because they do not believe in what they are saying or believe in the product they are pitching. It is a job and they are just going through the motions.

Jack was doing the same thing. He did not believe what he was saying. How could he? He was *not* Jack's Garbage Valet yet! So why did I not see that one coming? I should have started him out with our cans first. It would have been better if he did the work for a few weeks with us at home, and told him how great it was to know our cans were out and not worry about them.

When I saw him struggle, I encouraged him and gave him positive reinforcement. Even with the encouragement, I had to nag him to practice on me; he did not like it at first because it did not feel comfortable for him. He balked, but that was okay with me. I kept asking and each time his pitch got a little better! When he received his first "Yes", his attitude changed. You could see it in the way he carried himself. It was wonderful!

He kept asking me, "Why don't people just say 'Yes'?" It is a great service and they should *want* to do it."

This was a great opportunity to teach him about marketing and sales. How do you explain sales statistics to a 10 year old? You talk it though. Jack and I have a deal: He can ask me *anything*. I give him an answer and he can tell me if he does not understand. If he does not understand, he gives me a minute to think of a different way to say the same thing and we see if that version is understandable.

It might sound silly that we have outlined this process, but it has saved us from a number of arguments. I found when I would say something and could see he did not understand it; I immediately would say it another way. He would get frustrated with me for saying things over again in a different way. Actually, I made things *less* understandable; so we finally set some ground rules and now it works like a charm. In fact, it works so well sometimes Jack will say, "Mom, I didn't understand that. Can you explain it in a different way?" When that happens, I have to keep myself from smiling!

## Learning Marketing Cadence

Here is how I explained to Jack the relationship between marketing and sales. I explained to Jack when a company gives a sales pitch—whether it is telemarketing, advertising, or in-person sales—conventional marketing wisdom says it takes between five and seven impressions before a customer is ready and willing to purchase. I went on further to explain successful companies market to prospects (i.e., potential customers) on a regular basis. I have learned I get a much higher rate of understanding with Jack if I use simple real-world examples to bring home the point.

The day he asked me why people don't just jump at the idea of Jack's Garbage Valet, we were driving home from school. We had the radio on and it hit. I said to Jack, "If you needed to buy a mattress tomorrow, where would you go?"

He immediately started singing *Sleep Train, your ticket to a better night's sleep*, the local mattress store's jingle we hear on the radio all the time. Then I asked another question.

"How many times have you heard that commercial?"

"A million!"

"And, when you've heard it, how many times did you need to buy a mattress?"

"None!"

"What was the first thing that came to your mind when I told you that you needed to buy a mattress tomorrow?"

"That song."

"That is called 'marketing,' Jack!"

The look on his face was gratifying because I could tell from his express he really understood. He now knew why we were going out and putting more flyers on the cans in a couple of weeks. The concept of marketing cadence was something he now understood. He was also starting to understand the word "No" meant, "I am not interested in your product today," which does *not* mean they might not be interested in it tomorrow. Now he understands why we keep marketing—giving flyers—to the same people over and over; one day, they might say "Yes". Thank you, Sleep Train!

## *Building Confidence and Self-esteem*

Building confidence and self-esteem go hand and hand. They are very similar and—in my mind—are two halves to a whole. Confidence is having a belief in yourself and what you do; self-esteem is having enough belief in yourself and what you do that when others try to tear you down, you have what it takes inside to rise up and say, "I believe in myself and what I do, no matter what others say or do to me."

One of my favorite quotes is from Mark Twain. Twain said, "Keep away from people who try to belittle your ambitions. Small people always do that, but the really great make you feel that you, too, can become great."

This quote embodies what I try to teach Jack. Your ambitions are just that: *your ambitions.* When other people belittle us, they are trying to steal our ambitions. Whether it is a putdown on the playground or a colleague at work, it is the same thing. Putdowns come from bullies—young and old.

I cannot honestly say I have never put anyone down, treated a sales clerk badly or said something unkind. I do not think anyone can. However, one of the wonderful things about life is each day we start fresh. We have a brand new day to work on being the best version of ourselves we can be.

People will always try to steal our ambition, but *will we let them?* Learning how to handle rejection is a process, whether it is a customer saying, "No, thank you," or someone deliberately hurting your feelings. Learning how to bully-proof your self-esteem takes time and patience.

The more Jack sold his services, the more his self-confidence grew. Now, when you ask him what his business is, he can matter-of-factly rattle off his sales pitch. He has practiced a lot. One of the hardest things I have had to learn is to be patient when he is stuck. I have learned to let him try it get unstuck on his own, and I work hard at not jumping in to rescue him. Instead I try to only inject a word or two to help him get unstuck.

## Millionaire Skill #3: Love It

> *"Do what you love. Know your own bone; gnaw at it,*
> *bury it, unearth it, and gnaw it still."*
> —*Henry David Thoreau*

Once you "Dream It' and "Believe It", then you will naturally begin to "Love It". Jack loves having his own business and it has become part of him. He loves what he does and loves what it allows him to do.

He loves it on a number of levels:

- He loves helping his neighbors.
- He loves receiving money for his services.
- He loves seeing his bank account grow.
- He loves that this experience has allowed him to write a book to encourage other kids to start their own business.
- He loves the fact he is a published author.
- He loves and embraces the mission he has written for himself.

You have to love what you do or it is just a job. Talk to any nurse or firefighter and they will say they love what they do. They help people every day and love making a difference. Yes, it is a job, but they *Love It*. This is one of the perks of being an entrepreneur. You see a need, dream about filling it, believe your product or service is the best, and do it. You see the results of providing for your customers and you love what you do. The rewards are intrinsic and they feed on themselves.

My guess is, we have all hired or have been around someone who really does *not* love what they do. They do their job, but you can tell their heart is not in it. As a boss, I would rather hire someone who loves what they do; they come to work with a completely different attitude. Do they have off days like the rest of us? Yes, but an off day is different than being around someone who just plain does not want to be there. Are there days when the person who loves their job wishes they were fishing? Yes, but often their attitude is turned around by just being at the job—because they *love* what they do.

As a consumer what do I like? I like being around the person who loves what they do—they make me feel good about being their customer. What don't I like? I do not like being the customer of a person who does not like their job; it often makes me resent giving them money. It also makes me want to take my business elsewhere. I don't think I am special in my feelings here. I would wager most everyone feels the same way.

At first, Jack did not want to be a "Garbage Valet". He did not like the idea at all. He really thought it was a horrible idea and gave me more than an earful about it. It took a lot of cajoling to get him to agree to even try it. The lesson here is not easy. You have to know your kid. If they are going to hate the business, don't do it. You will completely defeat the process of teaching and undermine the entire process of learning the "Love It" millionaire skill. You will have to use your good judgment as well; if you think they will like it once they get started, give it a shot. Kids can be fickle. If you can figure out what they are objecting to, you have a shot at understanding the real reason they don't like something. Then you can make an educated guess and make the call as to whether to push for an idea or punt. What if you guess wrong? So what; guessing wrong is all part of the process and it is time to turn it into a wonderful teaching moment. Make a course correction and move on to the next great idea!

If you asked Jack now, do you like your business? He would tell you he *loves* it! He likes helping his neighbors. He likes what he is doing. If he had not tried—if I had let him dictate the course—he never would have known how much fun it would be.

## Millionaire Skill #4: Work It

> *"What we really want to do is what we are really meant to do. When we do what we are meant to do, money comes to us, doors open for us, we feel useful, and the work we do feels like play to us."*
>
> —*Julia Cameron*

Once you "Dream It", "Believe It", and "Love It", it is time to get out there and "Work It". This means taking the action step millionaires know they must do. We all have to get out of bed in the morning and make it happen. At times, this is going to be the hard part. With Murphy's Law in full swing, if it is possible for something to go wrong, it will!

Our job is to make sure the kids know they need to push through the issues and get the job done. For example, our garbage day is on Friday, so that means there are times when we want to go out of town but have to keep in mind Jack has a business and his customers are counting on him. Oddly enough, this is where being divorced has been a blessing. If Jack and I are going out of town, his dad will do his route. It does not happen often, but it does happen and it is great his dad is willing to pinch hit for his kid! Remember, the pinch hitter does not have to be a parent. It can be a good friend who is invested and believes in what you are doing with your kid and wants to help.

Another part about the "Work It" millionaire skill is teaching our kids to do the job in a way that over delivers to their customers. If their customers expect one thing, they need to go the extra mile. When their customer gives them feedback, they need to listen to the feedback with courtesy and do what their customer asks of them. This is all part of good customer service.

It is also an excellent opportunity to teach our kids negative feedback is not necessarily a reflection on them personally. Often, it is a course correction. If you teach them to take criticism with grace, you will have given them a decided leg up on most of their peers. Learning to not take things personally is hard; at any age. Even in my 50's there are times when I struggle with criticism. Be honest, be transparent and vulnerable with your kids; if they see you struggle, get up and dust yourself off, they will know they can do the same.

There are a million teaching moments and customer service examples out there! When you are in a store or in a situation where good customer service is given, make sure you recognize it. Discuss what happened with your kid, seek out the manager and give an "at-a-boy!" for the deserving employee.

Teach by example how to handle a sticky situation or how to stand up gracefully for your side of the argument. (Okay, so I am not *always* good at this one, but I try!) Talk about the good *and* bad things and ask how they would have handled the situation better or differently. Relate it back to their business and discuss what they would do in a similar situation.

As our kids begin to "Work It", a number of teaching moments will come up. Starting their own business will create opportunities for our kids to learn. The trick is to seize every one of those moments. I know I have done my job when Jack says to me, "Mom, can't there be *one* moment when you're not trying to *teach* me something?"☺

## Teaching Your Kids How to Shake Hands

*"The handshake is proper business protocol. Period."*
*—Barbara Pachtere*

Part of the sales pitch is introducing yourself to the person with whom you are speaking; and part of introducing yourself is shaking hands. The handshake is a very important part of the business world; how to conduct business is—after all—what we are teaching our kids.

The handshake is a nonverbal communication tool we use every day. It can convey confidence, sincerity and trust. How do you shake someone's hand? Do you have a soft handshake or a firm handshake? John Steinbeck said, "First impressions are lasting." If you have a wimpy handshake, please, *please* get out of your comfort zone and teach your kids to shake someone's hand with confidence. They do not have to squeeze the life out of it, or shake it up and down until their arm falls off—just teach them not to give a wimpy handshake.

Teach them the importance of making a good first impression by meeting someone's outstretched hand with confidence. Chances are, if our kids do not extend their hand first, most adults they meet will not extend their hand. Adults don't expect kids to shake their hand. Teach your kid to be the exception. Teach them to put their whole hand—not just part of it—out to the adults they meet and say, "Hi! My name is…"

I want to take a moment to talk about teaching this skill to young girls. It is especially important our young women learn this skill early. We are not holding court in Old England or meeting royalty—where you are supposed to put only your fingers out to shake, bow your head, and curtsy. We are in the twenty-first century where women are capable and contributing members in society and business. We need to teach our young women it is acceptable to assert themselves with confidence. Please don't confuse assertiveness with aggressiveness. These are two different forms of behavior.

In today's world women are an integral part of society, regardless of where they work, (in the home or outside the home); we are a vital part of the community. Women, like my mom, worked hard to achieve equal status. We need to honor the efforts of the women who came before us and broke down barriers. When we teach the young women of our society to conduct themselves in a confident manner, we are honoring all the women who came before us. I don't care what role you have chosen in life, being proud of who you are and your contributions is important.

Regardless of your gender, a proper handshake says, "Hello! It is good to meet you. I am interested in meeting you and having a dialog with you." Make no mistake; the first indication of one's sense of self worth is their handshake. If we teach our kids to shake with a wimpy handshake we are teaching them to show others they are less important.

In their book *The Handshake as Interaction,*[20] Peter and Dee Hall sum it up this way, "The handshake represents an expression of equality." In addition to an introduction, the handshake also closes a business deal by saying, "You have my word; I will do what I said I will do." It is an important part of both the opening and the closing of any conversation. Your handshake says, "My word is my bond." Teach your children to have a good, confident and steady handshake; they will thank you the rest of their lives.

20   Hall, Peter M. and Dee Ann Hall. *The Handshake as Interaction,* (Amsterdam: Mouton Publishers, 1983)

## *Teaching How to Make Eye Contact*

*"As an employer, I like to have a handshake from whoever I'm interviewing and to be looked in the eye. That tells me a lot at the very beginning."*

—*Carole Kolle*

Eye contact is another form of nonverbal communication used in the business world. It is an important way to show you are listening and their words are important to you. When we look down or look away, it can send a message we do not want to send.

I often work on this technique with Jack. I have been teaching him to look me in the eye for a long time. He still struggles with it at times, but it is a very important lesson to learn. Looking people in the eye when you talk to them can be hard if you are not used to it, so here are a few tricks to strengthen this important facet of communication.

- If you have trouble looking a person in the eye, focus on having eye contact while *they* are speaking. You can let your eye wander when you are talking, but, when they have the floor, bring your focus back to their eyes so they know you are listening and are interested.
- Make brief eye contact every few seconds rather than sustaining it over the whole conversation.

One thing that can help your kid more than anything is your insistence they look you in the eye when you talk to them. You should, in turn, look them in the eye. This modeling will help reinforce the importance of eye contact in a very personal way.

## *Teaching How to Speak with Confidence*

Speaking with confidence is a very important lesson. When kids learn this, they learn to believe in themselves. Encouraging kids to speak up is an important lesson at any age. You can help them practice by role playing. They will be better prepared and able to think on their feet if they have the luxury of practicing on you.

When Jack and I first walked around the neighborhood, we had fun with this. We put out flyers and he practiced on me. I had fun inventing outlandish things people might say, and he practiced how he would handle them. He soon realized, if he could handle what I was making up and throwing at him, he could handle anything because the truth was far easier than my fiction! It was fun and we laughed together at the situations I was churning out. I was trying to make it more like a fun game than learning. He now knows he can handle talking to someone older, which is important for school, social situations, and so much more.

## Strawberry Munching Monsters

After awhile, the bad dreams pillow trick wears off. It just doesn't work forever. When it stopped working I got creative. Jack's bad dreams seemed to always be haunted by monsters. With that same matter-of-fact look on my face, I explain monsters were not really mean or bad; they just looked scary so people assumed they were bad. They are not mean at all, as a matter of fact, they are very lonely. All monsters LOVE strawberries. If you see a monster in your dream all you have to do is feed the monster strawberries. They will know you want to be their friend and they will become your very best friend.

If your child is like mine, over time the monsters will become aliens. One night Jack told me he tried feeding the aliens in his dream strawberries, and it didn't work. The aliens were still mean. Once again I donned my matter-of-fact look and said, "Well of course it didn't work. Aliens HATE strawberries; but they LOVE marshmallows! Feed them marshmallows next time!"

It worked like a charm. At 12, Jack now knows the trick his mother played on him. I can't wait until he has his own kids and calls me up to tell me my trick worked like a charm! ☺

Learning to feel comfortable speaking to adults is something both my brother and I learned from our parents. By all standards, our folks were older when they married. When they married in 1952, Mom was 32 and Dad was 42. Back in the 50's, that was considered old to marry. As a result, our parents were more mature. They were adults and so were their friends and clients. As a result, we were often around people their age. They spoke to us as if we were adults, we ate the food they ate and were present when their friends were over. We were very lucky. As a result, we felt comfortable in our own skin and comfortable around adults. Growing up, I knew I was experiencing life in a different way from my friends. Most of my friends' parents were much younger and it was different. As I grew up, I could see the advantage my parents had given me. I followed in my parent's footsteps—in this regard. Jack has older parents and he was always encouraged and included in conversations with our friends and contemporaries. You can see the difference in how he carries himself around adults. You don't have to be an older parent to accomplish this with your kids. It is just a matter of teaching kids early how to speak to adults with respect and courtesy. Eye contact, handshakes and speaking so you can be heard are all skills we can teach our kids so they can show people respect and courtesy.

## Millionaire Skill #5: Own It

*"We have not passed that subtle line between childhood and adulthood until... we have stopped saying "It got lost," and say "I lost it."*

—Sidney J. Harris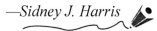

How many times has your kid told you, "It is not my fault!" Why is ownership such a difficult lesson? Taking responsibility is one of the most difficult of the six millionaire skills we have to teach our kids.

Millionaires do not run from responsibility. The first step in recovering from any mistake is to own it. You do this by looking someone in the eye and facing the issue head on. When you can admit your shortfall you own it. Once we do, we can determine where the mistake happened, and learn how to change the future by not making the same mistake twice. Setbacks or mistakes can be personal or circumstantial. We need to teach our kids admitting a mistake does not make them weak—on the contrary—if they take responsibility, they empower themselves. This is a hard lesson to teach. It is hard on two levels; how to teach it and how to react to it. To the first point, modeling "Own It" behavior to our kids can be one of the most powerful teaching tools we have in our parenting arsenal. The more we show our kids a willingness to admit our mistakes, the more likely they will be to "Own It" when they make a mistake. To the second point, the more we stand right by our kid's side when they have to *own* something, the better. Knowing they have our support and strength means a lot.

## Creating a Safe Place to Fail

> *"You always pass failure on the way to success."*
> —*Mickey Rooney*

We all fail, but how do we *handle* failure? Teaching our kids to shake it off and move on might be one of the kindest gifts we can give them.

When they fail, let them take a moment to feel their feelings. Let them experience what it's like to feel badly. It is okay to feel bad now and again. As parents we ache inside when our kids feel bad or hurt, but there are often lessons in those feelings.

One week, I went on a business trip—actually, it was a writer's conference—Jack's dad was in charge of taking Jack on his route. They successfully put the cans out, but they forgot to go the next day and put them back. I did not know this, and Jack did not realize it until we were driving home the next week and saw one of his customers. We pulled over to say hi and he said, "What happened last week?" After we talked, Jack and I realized he was telling us the cans didn't get put back the week I was gone. We explained Jack's dad had been helping him and they had forgotten to put the cans back. Jack apologized and said he would work on not letting that happen again. He held it together until we drove away and then the tears came. Jack's reaction to the mistake was palpable and I could not have been more proud of his reaction.

"I let them down!" he sobbed.

Did it kill me to have my son crying? Yes, but I used the mistake as an opportunity to reinforce the principles of responsibility. I let him feel the disappointment and we talked about it and used the incident to reinforce his commitment to his business and keeping his word. We also used it as an opportunity to reach out to his customers.

We wrote a letter to his customers, which he included with his next invoice, explaining what had happened. His customers were, of course, as gracious as they could be. In their reactions to his mistake, there was another lesson. We talked about understanding and recognized how they had given him a gift. We vowed to be patient with the next person who disappointed us.

We also talked about what Jack could do to make sure it didn't happen again. We worked out a plan. We came up with a couple of things. His school gives each kid a calendar date book at the beginning of each school year. We decided to write down in his date book on Thursdays: Cans Out and on Fridays: Cans In. If he was at home with his dad, he would see it and it would help the two of them remember. If he is out of town with me, we decided we would try to call his dad and remind him.

Jack is very lucky. His dad is very supportive of his business and helps him when he can. We are all human and frankly, when you don't do it every week it is easy to forget. Jack appreciates him for all he does for him with his business and he works on being as gracious to his dad as his customers are with him. All three of us work together to make sure Jack's garbage can route gets done, which is a good exercise in teamwork. It is good for Jack to see his divorced mom and dad work together on something for him.

## *Crossing the Cultural Divide*

> *"Nothing you do for children is ever wasted. They seem not to notice us, hovering, averting our eyes, and they seldom offer thanks, but what we do for them is never wasted."*
>
> —*Garrison Keillor*

I want to take a moment to address one of the most cherished realities about the U.S.: we live in a melting pot. People come to our country from all cultures to live the life of their dreams in freedom. Despite the fact we are a country made up of people from all cultures, in the short 200+ years this county has been in existence, we have managed to develop a unique U.S. culture.

For those from different cultural backgrounds, it presents the unique opportunity to help your kids learn two cultural norms. You are teaching one culture which is common and necessary in your home; and another culture—which may be contrary—but is the common cultural practice in the country where you live. You are very lucky. Your children can learn to be ambassadors of another culture to their friends—they can share two halves of a culturally rich and diverse whole.

My neighbor and best friend growing up was Suzette. Her mom was from El Salvador and her dad was from the U.S. Their home was a home with two cultures and I loved being there. Mrs. Mangan taught all her kids to speak Spanish and there were parties, music, dance and amazing food—their home was always full of life. It was wonderful and I was lucky enough to be an *adopted* part of their family. Even though Mrs. Mangan was born and raised in El Salvador, when she came to this country, she immersed herself in U.S. culture. She could toggle between her two worlds with ease and she was a stickler for the kids learning both cultures. They learned two ways to behave and conduct themselves—one in the "way of her country" and one in the way of the U.S. I always respected her for that and I cherish the lessons she taught me about "her culture".

There are several components in the act of talking to an adult which might go underappreciated. Multi-cultural families have such great learning opportunity in their homes; let's use eye contact as an example. In U.S., it is customary to look a person in the eye to establish confidence and convey your sincerity and truthfulness. In some Asian cultures, it is the complete opposite. It is common and polite—and a sign of respect—for children to keep their eyes cast downward and not look an adult in the eye. This is an example of where a parent makes a choice. They make the choice to be culturally responsive or culturally stubborn. Teaching your children how to navigate the ethnic traditions of those in the home and those in society is culturally responsive. Digging your heels in and saying, "This is the way it's done in my country" is being culturally stubborn.

Anyone who thinks kids don't naturally learn to navigate between two worlds is kidding themselves. Just look at how kids talk to their friends and how they talk to an authority figure. I'll use a classic Eddie Haskle quote to make my point. Eddie Haskle was a neighborhood friend of Wally Cleaver on the *Leave it to Beaver* TV sitcom—circa 1957—and was the quintessential self-seeking flatterer. The show centers around the Cleavers' youngest son—nicknamed Beaver (The Beav)—whose real name is Theodore. In the show, his brother Wally and his parents Ward and June Cleaver try to keep The Beav out of trouble. It was one of the first TV shows to be written from the kid's point of view and became an all-American icon. To set up the scene, Eddie and Wally are talking about going to the movies when Eddie finds out they have to drag Wally's little brother Beaver to the movies with them. He is not happy about this. In the middle of the discussion Mrs. Cleaver enters the room and in mid-sentence, Eddie changes the way he speaks—classic Eddie Haskle behavior. Eddie said, "Wally, if your dumb brother tags along, I'm gonna... Oh, good afternoon, Mrs. Cleaver. I was just telling Wallace how pleasant it would be for Theodore to accompany us to the movies." Yow! That boy could change on a dime—and so can our kids.

Let's face it, we all navigate between worlds. It is human nature, so teaching our kids early how to navigate two different cultures is not forsaking one's heritage—to me—it is actually respecting both. It might be out of someone's comfort zone, because it is not how they were raised, but it is such a gift. What do they say? "When in Rome, do as the Romans do!" In this section of the book, I base my suggestions on U.S. culture. When I co-author books for other cultures, and even co-author books for special needs kids, this section will be modified. Remember: if you reside in a culture where people speak to adults in a particular way, please modify my suggestions and guidelines so they are appropriate for the country in which you are living.

## Understanding How to Save

*"He who teaches children learns more than they do"*
*—German Proverb*

Jack walked a little taller after he opened his bank account. It is so much fun helping your kids do a simple thing like opening a bank account. I knew it was important to make sure he saved some of his money, so 70% in savings was part of the plan. I did not think watching his bank balance grow was going to be as exciting as it apparently was! For heaven sake, he gets excited when they post $.12 in interest! ☺

Make sure your kid knows to reinvest part of the money they save back into the business. I do not want to reinforce the "park and pray"[21] method of wealth building; however, I do want to temper the need to save with the need to reinvest in oneself and one's business.

Park and pray is a term coined by Loral Langemeier. It is the practice of parking your money in a traditional account and praying it grows rather than actively investing and managing your own wealth creation.

---

21 Loral Langemeier, *The Millionaire Maker's Guide to Creating a Cash Machine for Life*, (New York, NY: McGraw-Hill; April 2007)

Think big, dream big, and make it happen!

## Millionaire Skill #6: Give It

*"The value of a man resides in what he gives and not in what he is capable of receiving."*

—*Albert Einstein*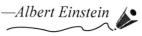

This is one of my favorite of the six millionaire skills: *Millionaires give back.* Millionaires realize the responsibility success carries and they give back. Some might give back monetarily; many give back with time and talent. The key is; the majority of millionaires give back to their communities.

The Spectrem Group is a consulting and marketing research firm that specializes in affluent markets. One of their recent studies show 96% of millionaires give to charity, which is higher than average.[22] Spectrum's report cites investors with $5 million to $25 million reported giving to charity. The average total was just over $13,200 a year.[23]

Here is the breakdown of exactly how millionaires tend to give:

---

22  Spectrem Group, *Millionaires and Mixed Trends in Charitable Giving*, (Chicago, IL: Spectrum Group; March 2011)

23  Spectrem Group, *Millionaires and Mixed Trends in Charitable Giving*, (Chicago, IL: Spectrum Group; March 2011)

Typical Yearly Charitable Contributions of Millionaires

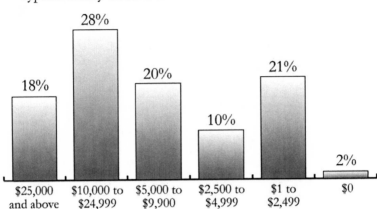

Source: Spectrem Group

More important than the money they donate, millionaires, who have a net worth of $1 million to $5 million, excluding their primary residence, gave *time*. They donated an average of 137 hours to charity each year with only 29% giving less than 40 hours a year and 30% giving 41 to 50 hours a year.[24]

The "Give It" millionaire skill is critical. It is important to teach our kids to give both their money and their time and talents. Jack is involved in scouting; community service is a component of the scouting program. Hundreds of websites suggest places to volunteer, including:

- Corporation for National & Community Service (www.serve.gov)
- VolunteerMatch (www.volunteermatch.org)
- Volunteer.gov: America's Natural and Cultural Resources Volunteer Portal (www.volunteer.gov)
- Habitat for Humanity (www.habitat.org)
- American Red Cross (www.redcross.org)

It does not matter what your passion is. Take your kids on a Saturday afternoon and just go out there and help! Giving of your time is such a wonderful experience and you get so much more than you give.

---

24  Spectrem Group, *Millionaires and Mixed Trends in Charitable Giving,* (Chicago, IL: Spectrum Group; March 2011)

In Chapter 1, I talked about changing our kids' conversations with money. Jack's conversation with money has significantly changed and now he is able to give. He started his business when he was 10 so, by his 11th birthday; he had been making about $50 a month for about nine months. This was enough time for him to see he had the ability to make money and spend it.

We were in the midst of planning his birthday party and I made the off-handed suggestion he might want to do something different this year.

"You know, Jack, you still have gifts in your closet from past birthdays you've never even opened. This year, instead of giving you a gift, why don't you ask people to donate money to a charity?"

Honestly, I did not expect this one to go over very well. I figured I would float it out there, he would completely dismiss it as one of the worst ideas I had ever come up with, and that would be that. Yet again, I was amazed by Jack's reaction.

"That's a *great* idea, Mom! I want my charity to be Operation Gratitude[25]!"

---

25  Operation Gratitude is a 501(c) (3) non-profit, volunteer-based corporation, funded entirely by private donations. For safety and security, the assembling of packages occurs at the Army National Guard Armory in Van Nuys, California.

Wow.

This would *never* have happened the year before. Jack would never have been able to see past the toys he would not get. He might have liked the idea, because he is a nice kid, but he would never have accepted the idea of giving up toys just for the satisfaction of giving. The very fact he could walk into a store and buy most any toy he wanted had changed the way he thought about money and giving. I was very proud.

We had his birthday party at a baseball game and invited family and friends. He was able to collect $595.00 in donations for Operation Gratitude! At the party, we had a letter writing station so our friends could write letters to soldiers. We collected checks and cash and sent it off to Operation Gratitude along with a letter explaining what he did and who contributed. They sent him a certificate, which he hung on the wall in his bedroom.

Jack and I do a lot of volunteering. I think it is important and Jack enjoys it, too, but that piece of paper on his wall really means something to him. For this year's party, he is going to have a donation drive again, but he has added a twist: We are having his party at home. It is going to be a movie night in our backyard and, in addition to asking for donations instead of gifts, he is asking people to bring old blankets to sit on and then leave behind. After we wash them, he wants to take them down to our local chapter of the Society for the Prevention of Cruelty to Animals (SPCA) and donate them to the shelter so the dogs and cats can have a clean, comfortable bed to sleep on while they are in the shelter.

After Jack's experience with his birthday, we decided we wanted to start a movement called *Make Your Birthday Matter*. We decided every kid has the opportunity to give back, whether for their birthday or some other reason. We established a website makeyourbirthdaymatter.com. It is a site where kids can go to get ideas for parties, read about other kids and what they are doing. They can register to tell us about the volunteering and charity work they are doing in their communities. It is not just about birthdays, but about celebrating kids who "Give It"!

Changing Jack's conversation with money has allowed him the freedom to give from the heart without any nagging sense he has to give up anything to do so. It is a powerful lesson.

This year, Jack came up with another new way to "Give It". Jack's dad and I made the decision Jack would not play baseball in Little League this year. He was in a new school and the workload was different. Between his struggles with Dyslexia and all the changes in his life, we did not think the rigors of the baseball season would be a good thing for him.

However, he did still love baseball, so he and his dad umpired a few games; something they started the year before. The kids who umpired were paid. It was not much—something between $15 and $25—depending on what position they umpired. Jack decided he wanted to donate the money he received back to Little League. I was very proud of this idea and was pleased he was continuing to seek new ways to "Give It"!

## *More Benefits Than You Can Imagine*

Jack has learned many more things in this venture than just those I have listed. Our relationship, which was already very strong, has grown even stronger. We have enjoyed doing something productive together rather than something we *have* to do, like homework. I get just as excited as he does when he gets a new customer. We work together on his business. I am out there with him, helping drag cans in or out or using the weed whacker and it is a positive experience for both of us.

When you start this venture with your kid, I am confident you will find a completely new set of benefits I have not even mentioned. On our website, howtoraiseamillionaire.com, I have set up a section for you to share your experiences. Please visit our site, click on the *Share It* button on the home page, and tell us what you have experienced with your kid. You can inspire others, give tips, and tell us about fun antics you and your kids are sharing.

Mother Teresa said, "I am a little pencil in the hand of a writing God who is sending a love letter to the world." If that is the case, then we—parents—are a pen in the hand of our children as they compose the wishes and dreams of their lives. What we do and say is written in ink. How and what we teach our kids is hard to erase. It takes a lot to overcome the impressions we parents leave on the souls of our children. I—for one—want the impressions I leave on Jack's soul to be the most positive and inspirational messages possible.

I want Jack to "Dream It", "Believe It", "Love It", "Work It", "Own It", and "Give It" with all the positive and uplifting energy he can muster!

---

There is just no way to make this subject a happy one. I never thought I would find myself in the position where I was getting a divorce.

It was surely one of the hardest things I have had to go through in my life.

I am, however, proud to say that through the entire process, I worked very hard to keep my personal feelings in check and do what needed to be done to put Jack first.

My motto was and is:

I am a mom first and a divorced person second.

Should you find yourself in the unfortunate position of going through a divorce, I hope some of these resources can help you. There is a little something for everyone on this page. I hope find some of these resources helpful.

**www.howtoraiseamillionaire.com/divorce**

*Chapter 4*

# Grass Grows, Dogs Poop, and the Garbage Man Cometh!

*"Whatever the mind of man can conceive and believe, it can achieve. Thoughts are things! And powerful things at that, when mixed with definiteness of purpose, and burning desire, can be translated into riches."*

—*Napoleon Hill*

## *Picking the Right Business for the Right Reason*

You do not have to go any further than your own neighborhood to come up with a viable business idea for your kid, such as babysitting, odd jobs for neighbors, or vacation house sitting. These are great supplemental jobs, but they all lack something critical and not often considered when picking a business for a kid: cash flow.

"Lady, you want my kid to think of *cash flow*? Isn't that a bit *much*?"

No, it is not. It might be more than most people think of, but it is a critical piece to the success of any business. Remember, you are working on setting your kids up to succeed. They need to learn early how to evaluate things on an unemotional basis. When you teach your kid about running a business, cash flow had better be part of the equation. You are not teaching them how to: *do a job*. You are teaching them how to: *run a business*. A business has to have cash flow to keep its doors open, pay the electricity, make payroll and keep the water flowing.

## Creating a Cash Machine

> *"Positive thoughts get reinforced through positive action, and negative thoughts through negative action. It's an incredibly simple concept to understand, but takes a lot of patience and persistence to get right, and you have to stick with it."*
>
> — *Loral Langemeier*

In Loral Langemeier's best-selling book, *The Millionaire Maker's Guide to Creating a Cash Machine for Life*,[26] she talks about how to create a steady "cash machine." I love this term because it is so accurate. I read this book and loved her philosophy.

It describes a way to change your thinking about your assets. Whether you agree with this model or not, it is a great metaphor, so let's think about how we can apply the *cash machine* concept to our kids' businesses.

Why do kids like allowance? They like allowance because they get it every week—like clockwork. It is a *cash machine*. Or—should I say—*you* are a *cash machine*. I want to change this. When you think about what kind of business

---

26  Loral Langemeier, *The Millionaire Maker's Guide to Creating a Cash Machine for Life*, (New York, NY: McGraw-Hill; April 2007)

to start with your kid, it is important for them to think of a business that can be "the gift that keeps on giving"—a cash machine. That is why my idea for Jack was such a good one. (Yes, I am going to take full credit and glory on this one. I thought of a great idea!)

Notice how I didn't say "When your kid thinks about what kind of business to start", but instead said, "When you think about what kind of business to start with your kid". Trust me, this will be their business in name only. It is really a joint venture. This will be a joint venture with all the cash going into your kid's pocket and the intangibles going into your pocket. We'll talk more about how this process is going to morph you from parent to Trusted Advisor. Now back to the business at hand

As I mentioned in Chapter 2, I thought of Jack's Garbage Valet when he was about seven years old. As I said, he was not keen on the idea at first, and it literally took me a full three years to get him to warm up to the idea. When he warmed up to the idea of starting a business I had that little hurdle of perception to overcome. I knew the reason *I* thought the Garbage Valet business was such a great idea; I had to teach Jack to think like a true entrepreneur and see past the task to the heart of the business: the cash machine. Garbage Valet, Grocery Valet, Pet Pooper Valet, Lawn Manicurist and the like are all great jobs. The garbage man comes once a week, people regularly need groceries, lawns grow and pets poop! If you can come up with a consistent weekly or monthly need, you are "made in the shade".

Some businesses have drawbacks:

- Lawn service (mowing) is good, but only those with lawns need it. It is time consuming, requires a mower, is somewhat physical, and, if you live in a place with snow or four distinct seasons (where grass only grows part of the year), it is a limited source of income.
- Baby sitting is a good business, but it requires your customers have kids and they have to want to go out. This can be limiting. Mind you, I did a lot of babysitting when I was young and it makes great ancillary income. It is not, however, the most reliable cash machine.

Here are some better ideas:

- Pooch Valet or a dog-walking service is good for city dwellers who walk their dogs in the morning. Remember: people with dogs tend to spend money on their four-legged family members.
- Pet Pooper Valet is also a good business, but it requires your neighbors have dogs. This limits the number of potential customers and since this is a numbers game, it makes it harder.
- Grocery Valet is a great inner-city service, which can actually be two types of service:

  You can offer a shopping service where you would pick up your customer's list, go to the store once a week—or more, if needed—and shop for their groceries. Most of us have neighbors who have a hard time getting around or are very busy. This service would require a little more hands-on work from an adult, but think of all the things your kids can learn. Imagine going back to your customers and saying, "I know you like Dole Pineapple, so I clipped this coupon and saved you $.50 today!" ☺

  You can offer to carry groceries home from the grocery store. This valet service is ideal for inner cities where people have to carry their groceries to flats or apartments. Get a wagon and offer to carry them to the door and then inside. Senior citizens who need a little help would welcome this service.

The critical part is to create a cash machine. Think of services your kid can offer that have a regular cadence of every week or month. This is the key to success from a cash flow perspective as well as a kid-friendly perspective. If you make a business that is too infrequent, your kids will get bored and lose interest. If it is something they know they have to do every week, they will look forward to doing it and get greater and more consistent satisfaction from the doing!

## *Diversifying Your Kid*

> *"Most people never get wealthy simply because they are not trained financially to recognize opportunities right in front of them. The rich have learned to recognize opportunities as well as how to create them."*
>
> —*Robert Kiyosaki*

Once your kid has figured out their core business, they can add ancillary income, which is vital. In business, a one trick pony does not usually survive, so this is a valuable lesson. Some examples of ancillary incomes are pet sitting, vacation mail retrieval, holiday light decoration installation, yard watering (whether during a vacation or in veggie season), babysitting, spring weed pulling and light "honey-do" jobs.

You do not have to limit the ancillary work to your existing customers. They are simply the "low-hanging fruit"; they know your child's business and they know your child. They have developed a level of trust and offering them other services is natural; however, do not let this prevent you from putting the other services onto a flyer the next time you have one to deliver. People in the neighborhood might need someone to fulfill other services, and it is great to let them know your kid is out there. The next time they have a nagging job they do not want to do, they might just call your young entrepreneur to do it for them!

Another thing to consider is putting a quote from a customer about a particular ancillary service on your flyer. So far, Jack has done vacation mail, pet sitting and vacation yard care for his customers. In one of his flyers, we have a quote from a customer about vacation mail and pet sitting. It is a great way for his prospects to hear from fellow neighbors about his service.

## Under Promise and Over Deliver

Ancillary businesses have also allowed me to teach Jack the business principle of *under promise and over deliver*. This is real simple. The idea is when you do a job; you do the job beyond what the customer expects. An example of this is when Jack was asked by one of his customers to water their garden, while they were on vacation. When we went to their backyard, for the first time, you could see how they loved their yard. The perennial garden they had planted was just beautiful. But beyond the plants and trees, a number of tools were out, leaves had fallen from a big tree and there were other small things Jack could do to freshen up their yard.

I could see opportunity was knocking for another teaching moment. I talked with him about what they expected him to do while they were on vacation. We talked about how nice it would be for them to come home to a clean and organized backyard. We talked about how building customer loyalty was critical and how if he put extra effort into the job they had given him; he could not only create a satisfied customer, but they would most likely tell their neighbors about him.

He set about working on those extra things each day. One day he raked leaves. Another day he picked up the tools and put them all in one place. Another day he hosed off the walkways. He did the extra work over the time they were gone and by the time they came back, their backyard was all spiffed up and looking fantastic. He could not wait for them to get home! He was so very proud of what he had done and their reaction was the pay off. He under promised and over delivered.

---

# The ? Box

This is a new pearl we are trying and came to me from one of my Noble moms, Amy.

As Jack matures and becomes a teenager, he often has questions he is uncomfortable asking in person. I want him to know he can ask those questions of me. I know first-hand some of the whoppers he gets from school; I would rather he gets the straight scoop. We have a box called "The ? Box". It is actually a small mailbox, about 3 inches x 2 inches. It has a little flag like a real mailbox, which makes it easy for me to see when there is a question in the box. It sits in our kitchen. Jack is free to put any question in the box; any question.

Once his question is in the mail box, he puts the flag up; signaling to me there is a new question. I retrieve the question, answer it, put it back in the box and put the flag down; signaling to him his question has been answered. This might seem like a lot of gyrations to go through for some simple questions, but Jack knows I'll answer his question truthfully and he still keeps his privacy. This is also another step towards the Trusted Advisor status. When he gets older and these maturity questions are not quite so new and embarrassing, he may—or may not—get to the point where the box is not necessary. For now, he keeps his anonymity (OK—sort of) and still gets his questions answered.

---

## Factors to Consider When Starting a Business

Several factors come into play when we are brainstorming with our kids about what business to start. We have to be practical. If a great opportunity becomes available, say "Yes" and figure it out later; however, make sure it is not over your kid's head. Pick a business that will work logistically for you and—at the same time—be careful not to set your kid up for failure.

Here are some factors to consider:

- **Think about your life's schedule.** Think about how much time you will need to dedicate to this venture.
- **Think about timing.** When would they be doing this job and when would you need to help them? Chances are you'll do this job together so make sure you have carved out time in your schedule too.
- **Think about the tools you will need.** If you need a wagon to collect groceries, make sure you have one or can have access to one quickly.

- **Put the brakes on the number of customers your kids should get.** Make sure the business grows along with them; do not let the business outgrow their ability and developmental skills. Having one customer makes a business. If that is what you start out with and can handle, great. Grow it when your child is ready. In the back of your mind, know how much time each customer takes. Make sure the amount of work is appropriate for their age and then grow accordingly. When we first started, Jack could handle about four customers with no problem. As he grew and matured, we actively added more customers. Now, at 12, he is ready to add more, so we will put on a campaign to add about five more customers by a certain time.

We take it slow and are not in a hurry to get too big before he can handle it. And more importantly, we talk about it. We discuss the growth of his business together. I am not the great Oz pulling the levers behind the curtain. He is fully involved and invested. This is how he learns. We have open discussions about what we—together—can handle with his schedule (homework, music lessons, scouting, etc.). These are all factors we take into consideration.

Our kids can do more than they think, so do not hamper them by making them think they cannot handle something. Jack has a goal of adding three new customers this year. I think he can handle an additional five easily, so I thought his goal of three was great. My hope—and parental plan—is he will blow past that goal and be over the moon with his success. This helps to reinforce the idea of goal setting; going past his goal encourages him to believe in himself and strive for more!

In Chapter 7, I will describe a five-day plan on how to start a business. In the five-day plan, Day 1 focuses on picking the right business for your kid. I also provide additional resources in our Fast Start Action Guide, which includes fun exercises you can do together to start the brainstorming process.

## Embracing Your New Relationship with Your Kid

Prepare yourself: your relationship with your kid is going to change. When you correctly brainstorm and do collective thinking with your child, it will show them a different side of you. Your parenting will morph into a different level. You will open them up to the idea that—together—you can solve any problem, tackle any challenge, and come out winners. It is powerful and fun.

You will lay a foundation and establish a precedent as a *Trusted Advisor*, which they can then carry through their difficult teen years. You will not be just the "Yes" and "No" parent but the Trusted Advisor to whom they can go when they need to figure out a problem. You will be the person they trust to help them through a crisis.

Frankly, you will be changing your parenting position and taking on a new and more powerful role with your child. I am not advocating you abdicate your primary role as parent; instead, I am suggesting you can take on the *additional* role of Trusted Advisor. I am not suggesting you be their buddy or friend; instead, I am saying, by showing your child how to start their own business, your street credibility will increase and they will begin to come to you with questions only a Trusted Advisor can answer.

Be wise. Think—do not react. Use every ounce of restraint you have to thoughtfully answer Trusted Advisor questions when you get them. Lay out options and guide them to pick a course of action of which you will both be proud. Advisors are not dictators. As our kids transition from middle childhood to teenage years, they crave control. When a Trusted Advisor lays out choices, with pros and cons fully explored; informed choices can be made. Teaching our kids to make informed choices is the powerful stuff adulthood is made of. I want to be there to help Jack navigate through the troubled waters of his teenage years. I know there will be plenty of times when he won't come to me; but my hope is the tools I am teaching him will be ones he uses—on his own—to make informed decisions.

I want to tackle another topic many people find hard to talk about with their kids. I don't know one parent who wants their kids to get involved with drugs and alcohol, but often we handle this subject in a dictatorial fashion.

We think telling our kids not to do it will cut it. Well often it won't and often it will have the opposite effect.

My Cub Scouts and their parents know I am big on talking openly about this stuff. I wanted to devote a page to giving you resources you can use to open the lines of communication. Courage my fellow parents—this is the kind of stuff that really counts!

I hope you find these often candid resources useful.

**www.howtoraiseamillionaire.com/open**

*Chapter 5*

# Five Practical Business Skills

*"Success is neither magical nor mysterious. Success is the natural consequence of consistently applying the basic fundamentals."*

—*Jim Rohn*

## What Kids Need to Know and How to Teach It

Before we get started with the five-day plan in Chapter 7, I wanted to give you an overview of what we are teaching the kids and then offer some tips on how to do it. It is important you have the end game in mind. When situations present themselves, it is easier to think *on the fly* if you remember the end game.

The whole point of helping your kid start a business is to give you the opportunities to instill the six millionaire skills: "Dream It", "Believe It", "Love It", "Work It", "Own It" and "Give It". As you teach the fundamentals of business to your child, keep those skills in mind and reinforce them as often as you can. Bring all situations back to these six skills whenever possible. Call the skills by name, and use the skill titles often so they become a part of your child's vocabulary. The more you use them, the more the skills will become second nature. The more you can make these skills an involuntary response, the better.

As we have previously discussed, from a more practical perspective, you will teach your child the following business skills:

111

- Marketing and Sales
- Accounting
- Execution
- Customer Service
- Follow-up

If your initial reaction is to think your kids are too young to learn these skills, you are dead wrong. Our kids are more sophisticated than we realize. Do not sell them short. Simply explain what these things are in terms they can understand. Relate the lessons to something they are familiar with and they will jump on board faster than you thought possible.

If you have never owned or managed a business, these skills might seem a little out of your league, but nothing could be further from the truth. The fact is anyone can learn all the required skills to run a business. They are not rocket science but instead are practical and common sense.

Case in point: early in my marketing career, I worked for a small start-up company whose product was a multidimensional database. Our target audience was chief financial officers (CFOs). We offered many half-day seminars and sent out invitations to CFOs at companies the same size as our own. I thought the invitations—letter style and personalized to each CFO— were very expensive, so I tried to get the Director of Marketing to change to an oversized postcard format; I thought we had a better chance of these CFOs reading a postcard than opening an envelope. Unfortunately, I did not have any data to support my theory—just my own belief. The way I looked at it, if I got a letter in the mail from a company I did not know, I would probably toss it; believing it to be junk mail without opening it. What makes me think I am so different from a CFO? Nothing.

However, I knew my personal habits were not enough to change this well-oiled machine, so I went to our CFO, explained I was new and wanted to do some research. I asked him to keep all the mail he received at work, mark on the outside if he opened it or not, and why. If it was something he needed, I asked him to save only the envelope and note why he opened it. I did not tell him what I thought he would do or let him know why I was doing it because I did not want to taint the results in any way. I told him it was just research to help me do my job better.

He willingly agreed to help and he did this for a number of weeks. I would occasionally go into his office and ask if he was still doing it. He would smile and say, "Yes!" At the end of my experiment, I got the mail from him. He graciously went through each piece and explained his notations.

"I didn't open this one because I didn't know who these people were. I opened this one because it was from a law firm, but it was junk mail."

My unscientific research showed:

- He got a lot of mail.
- He never opened anything from anyone he did not know because he assumed it was junk mail.
- He read the postcards if they had a picture or slogan that caught his eye.

After he went through all the mail, I explained my request. I told him the marketing department had always sent invitations in a personalized envelope with a personalized cover letter and an enclosed invitation. I told him I thought this method was too expensive and ineffective, but I did not have empirical data to back up my theory so I had used him as my data.

He was floored! He said he had never had anyone from marketing ask him for help. He thought it was cool and, I have to admit, it *was* cool! Naturally, I could not have been more pleased with the outcome. After all, it supported my theory.

As a result, I was able to convince the marketing department to follow my suggestion and try—just *try*—my postcard idea. We got more responses and had more attendees at those seminars then we had ever had. We never went back to the other invitations (at least not while I was at the company) and our expenditures for printing and postage were literally cut in half.

This story illustrates it does not take a Master of Business Administration degree to figure out marketing. In the case of my story, it was not hard to figure out why we were struggling to get "cheeks in our seminar seats". People were not reading our invitations!

I just looked at my own habits and said, "I don't waste my time opening envelopes from strange companies with barcodes across my name that scream JUNK MAIL! What makes me think a busy CFO would?" I do, however, glance at cool postcards that catch my eye, and see what they are sending me. Am I so different from the CFO sitting down the hall from me? The point is anyone can do this stuff; you just have to try.

Likewise, if you are a business owner or professional, you might be thinking, she can't teach me anything. You might very well be correct. Maybe I can't teach you a darn thing. Maybe you know everything there is to know about business. But then maybe—just maybe—I can. I came up with clever ways to teach my kid how to understand and implement a business model. Regardless, have an open mind and see what the next few chapters bring. If I can help you with one idea, I will be thrilled.

As you put your child's business plan into action, and begin to think about these areas of business, think about your everyday experiences and remember to relate those experiences back to your kid when you are trying to explain these advanced concepts. We experience these five business skills every day; maybe it is when we go to our mailbox, maybe it is when we enter a store, listen to the radio, or watch TV. There is hardly a time when we are not experiencing some aspect of someone's business. The trick is for you and your kids to increase your awareness, become more in tune with what is going on around you, and identify the experience with a business skill.

## Business Skill #1: Marketing and Sales

*"Old marketeers never die, they just get promoted."*
—*Ann Morgan James*

Marketing and sales surround us every day. Some happen at the same time; some may happen in a particular order. Here are nine steps of a typical sale, and we will talk about how to teach each of them to your kid. The words in parenthesis after the titles below tell you how Jack did this in his Garbage Valet business.

### Sales Cycle: The Nine Steps of Making a Sale

1. **Introduce yourself and get to know your potential customer** (done with flyer).

   This first step to the sales cycle might seem obvious, but the point is to help your kid understand they need to let their potential customers know they are out there and available. If they do something fun and catchy, their customers will remember them.

2. **Tell your potential customer about your service or product** (done with flyer and in person with your sales pitch).

   While the majority of your customers will get your flyer and read it, some people are outside and you will meet them while you are delivering your flyers. For those neighbors (and others), you will need to have a quick few sentences—not the details, but just a quick overview—to explain what you do. We call this the "high-level sales pitch" or the "30,000-foot sales pitch".

   Here is Jack's "high-level sales pitch":

   > "Hi! My name is Jack James. I am your neighbor and I live on XYZ Street. Are you getting tired of taking your garbage cans in and out? Then hire me! For $10 a month, I'll take your cans in and out and you won't have to worry anymore."

   Remember: This is something your kids will need to practice before it comes naturally and easily. The hard part is letting them do it when they get tongue-tied and flustered. Remember; give little hints to help them get it right instead of saying it for them. You will have to bite your tongue sometimes but, if you do, the words will soon be sailing out of them!

3. **Ask your potential customer if they have ever had the problem your product or service solves** (done with flyer or in person).
Learning to ask is an art. As discussed in Chapter 1, teaching kids how to ask can be an empowering skill. In *The Aladdin Factor,*[27] Jack Canfield and Mark Victor Hansen offer the suggestion of using The 8 Principles of Asking:

1. Ask as if you expect to get it.
2. Ask with conviction.
3. Ask someone who can give it to you.
4. Be clear and specific.
5. Ask from your heart.
6. Ask with humor and creativity.
7. Give in order to get.
8. Ask repeatedly.

If you can help your children master these eight principles, they will become masters at asking. They will also learn an important flipside of asking. They will acquire the understanding "No" is a common answer and learn how not to take it personally—an important step in bully-proofing their self-esteem.

4. **Ask your potential customer to buy your services or product** (done with flyer and in person).
Being a sales person is a hard job. Frankly, it is an art. I have always been impressed by people who are in sales and I have had my share of opportunities to work with sales reps because of my marketing business. I specialize in Field Marketing which is marketing specifically done in the field; directly to the prospects for the benefit of the sales reps. The sole purpose of Field Marketing is getting someone in the sales pipeline. Of course, when you do a field marketing campaign you naturally achieve things like awareness, but the primary purpose is to market closer to the prospect so you can get them to put their big toe into the sales cycle. The sales rep takes it from there.

---

27    Jack Canfield and Mark Victor Hansen, *The Aladdin Factor,* (Niles, IL: Nightingale Conant, 2000)

In all the years I have worked with sales reps, what continues to impress me is the ability of a good rep to shake off the "No". Sales reps run the gamut as far as ability, just like any other profession, and when you meet a good one, you know it. In my opinion, the success of any rep is directly proportional to their ability to take the "No" and move on. Do they take "No" as the last time they speak to them? Nope, they go back, each time there is an opening because they know most people are going to tell them "No" several times before they say "Yes". This subject is so important it is worth looking at a little research to back up my assertions.

These assertions are legitimized by various studies, but I like the work of the researchers for the Behavioral Sciences Research Press the best. They have studied and dissected the art of sales for more than 25 years—from a number of aspects. The president and CEO, Shannon Goodson, wrote an amazing book along with the firm's chairman, George Dudley called *The Psychology of Sales Call Reluctance: Earning What You're Worth.*[28] They interviewed over 100,000 salespeople to try to understand what made some successful and others not. Their findings were complex and detailed, but simply put:

- 80% of all new salespeople fail because of "call reluctance".
- 40% of all veterans stop prospecting because of "call reluctance".

The term "call reluctance" is one they coined and it means simply: being reluctant to make a sales call. It can be the result of a number of factors or fears. Regardless, the result remains the same. The average sales rep will make 5 times less money if they are call reluctant.[29]

28  George W. Dudley and Shannon L. Goodson, *The Psychology of Sales Call Reluctance: Earning What You're Worth in Sales,* (Dallas, TX: Behavioral Sciences Research Press, May 1999)

29  Dudley, George W. and John F. Tanner Jr., *The Hard Truth About Soft-Selling,* (Dallas TX: Behavioral Science Research Press, 2005)
Tanner, John F. Jr., George W. Dudley, and Lawrence B. Chonko, *Salesperson Motivation and Success: Examining the Relationship between Motivation and Sales Approach,* (San Antonio TX: Advances in Marketing: Managerial, Pedagogical, Theoretical Conference, November 2005)

Why am I spending so much time on sales? It is critical to the success of your kid's business. When you start this venture, you are going to be naturally all pumped up about it. You are going to work on your kid and get them all excited about the prospect of starting their own business. When it does not meet expectations, it is you who will have to keep the ship afloat and steaming ahead. It is going to be natural for your child to want to quit. Why? Because starting a business is not easy. It takes work! We all want stuff to be easy. When we can't see the reward right in front of our face, we need something to keep us going. If you understand the science behind successful sales, you can explain to your kids why they need to be patient; you can scientifically explain it. This is not you, it is research telling them. Trust me—they will believe it much faster if it is not just your opinion. This is all part of the "Work It" millionaire skill. It is what sets millionaires apart. They don't give up—they are not daunted by people telling them "No", they just say, "Next".

Here are a few more data points for you to keep in your pocket:
- 46% of salespeople ask for the order only once before giving up

- 24% ask twice before they are scared off and call reluctance rears its ugly head and they give up
- 14% give it a third shot, then they just plain give up
- 12% actually make it to a fourth try before they throw in the towel

Here is the kicker! The research from this study showed that *60% of all sales were made after the sales reps had asked five times or more.* By my math calculations, that is 4% of the people getting 60% of the sales.

What percent do you want your kids to be in?

We can inoculate our kids against being afraid to hear the word "No" by letting them hear it repeatedly and realize it is acceptable to hear it. Remember: They are going to hear "No" 20 times before they hear "Yes". Help them learn to ask people to buy so they can be a success!

5. **Seal the deal with a handshake** (done in person).

In Chapter 3, we talked about the art of the handshake, which is also an important part of learning about integrity. The Aspen Institute and Booz Allen Hamilton Inc. invited approximately 9,500 worldwide senior executives to participate in a global research study to understand how companies manage values.[30] When these executives were asked about their corporate values, the #1 and #2 answers were "ethical behavior/integrity" and "commitment to customers," broken down as follows:

| | |
|---|---|
| Ethical Behavior/Integrity | North America: 95% <br> Europe: 84% <br> Asia/Pacific: 85% |
| Commitment to Customer | North America: 87% <br> Europe: 90% <br> Asia/Pacific: 86% |

*Source: The Aspen Institute and Booz Allen Hamilton*

---

30  Chris Kelly, Paul Kocourek, Nancy McGaw, Judith Samuelson, *Deriving Value from Corporate Values,* (McLean, VA: The Aspen Institute and Booz Allen Hamilton Inc., 2005)

Teaching our kids their word means something is a very critical life lesson. When we teach them to shake hands with a customer, it brings home the point they have made a commitment they must keep. Talk to them about what it means to give their word. Talk about how integrity and trust are important values in business and in life. This is an integral part of the "Own It" millionaire skill.

6. **Deliver your product** (done in person).

I have said it before; this is where the rubber meets the road. Be kind to yourselves. It takes time to get into the swing of things, so know that going in. Please, *please* understand it is your responsibility to make sure they succeed! Remind them, be there, take them out and help them do their job.

Do not think teaching them through failure is the best way. *It is not!* Sure, there are times when we all learn lessons the hard way, but this is not one of them. Remember: you are working to become their Trusted Advisor and to be trusted, you have to have their back!

It is also important to remember anyone can do a job or task right or wrong; your responsibility as the parent is to help your kids strive to do their best. Teach them to over deliver. For example, if their customer is home and you see the newspaper in the driveway or mail in the mailbox, have your child deliver it to them personally. Tom Peters, world renowned business consultant, says, "Formula for success: under promise and over deliver." I am not suggesting you teach your kids to sandbag people; instead, teach them to go a step beyond what is expected.

7. **Ask for the money** (done in person and with your invoice).

This is where your kids will have some fun! It is such a thrill to get paid for the first time. Remember: the first few times your kid asks for money, it needs to be done in person. Remind them to use their best manners and thank their customer. You will be surprised at how having cold hard cash handed to them will suddenly make all those hours you spent saying, "Say thank you!" go right out the window! They will completely forget their manners; you'll need to gently remind them.

Remind your kids to ask their customers:

- Is there is anything else I can do for you?

- How can I improve my service?
- Do you know if any of your neighbors need my services?

These questions teach your kid how to improve and expand their business *intelligently*. If a neighbor says they occasionally need someone to pick up their mail while they are out of town, you now know you can offer this service to your neighbors and someone is likely to need it. A good businessperson does customer research—asking questions about what other services they can provide—to understand the needs of their customers.

Do you remember my story in Chapter 2 about being bad at invoicing? Please do not follow my lead. Find an easy accounting method from the start and go with it. Find what works and help your kid be a success at the accounting end of the business.

8. **Ask for a referral** (done with flyer or in person).

   Asking for referrals is a great way to get new customers. It is also a great way to follow up those customer service questions. If your customer gives you a nice compliment after you ask them how you did, it is a great time to say, "If you like my service, I would really appreciate you referring me to one of your neighbors."

Chances are it never occurred to them to refer you! When you ask them to do it, they often do. The other thing you can do is ask if you can quote them on your next flyer. How powerful to have a customer's quote to show prospective customers! It is also a nice compliment to your customer. It says to them; I value your opinion.

9. **Reward your customers for their referral** (always done in person).

   While you are asking your customers for referrals, define your referral reward program. Some people need added incentive, so accommodate them! Besides, it is just plain nice!

   As I mentioned in Chapter 2, Jack's referral program is a $5 Starbucks gift card for any referral that signs up for his service. This gets people to tell their neighbors about Jack and rewards them when one of their referrals turns into a customer.

## *Marketing with Flyers*

Now that we have defined and have an understanding of the sales cycle, we will look at how marketing dovetails into the picture. Pick an example to drive home the marketing message you are trying to get across to your kid, such as my Sleep Train example from Chapter 3. After you help your kid decide what business to start, walk them through the sales cycle and then decide how to market it.

As we discussed in Chapter 2, one of the easiest ways to get the word out to your neighborhood is with flyers. As you and your child build your first flyer, make sure it contains these critical elements:

- Identify the problem
- Describe how your service or product fixes the problem
- Define how much you charge for this service
- Provide your business name
- Include your contact information

If your flyer includes humor and creativity, it will be memorable. We always include Jack's picture with his flyer so our neighbors will recognize him. We all like to do business with people whom we know and trust. While most of our neighbors did not know Jack when he started out, it didn't take long for many of them to start saying, "Hey! You're the kid on that flyer, aren't you?" His picture went a long way to making his flyer memorable. Never underestimate the power of a picture; when was the last time you got a flyer from a real estate agent that *didn't* have their picture on it? They put them on their flyers for a reason.☺

## *Business Skill #2: Accounting*

Chapter 2 explains how we did our accounting. Now we will talk about some of the important concepts you need to teach in the process.

In order to run a business, a basic understanding of "revenues" and "expenses" is required; after that, you can continue by teaching them additional concepts including "assets" and "liabilities." The idea is to teach your kid how to keep a positive cash flow—not turn them into accountants. Make sure they understand money goes in and money goes out.

I encourage you to open a savings account for your child. When we opened one for Jack, he loved it! As I said before, there is nothing as fun as watching your child's thrilled face as the teller enters the $.04 interest in their account book.

At some point you'll want to help them open a checking account. As your kids mature it will be important for you to teach them how to balance a checkbook. When the nonprofit Jump$tart Coalition for Personal Financial Literacy surveyed 12th graders, they found only 10% could satisfactorily answer questions about personal finance.[31] Did you get that? *10% of 12 graders*!

These same young people will be out earning a living very soon! Many of them are 18 and can vote, but they do not understand personal finance. If you do not help your kids learn how to budget, write checks and balance a personal checkbook, they will not know how to do it when they leave home. These important accounting skills learned in their business will help them in many areas.

The amount of time you spend in this area is up to you, but I suggest you give them a solid education in invoicing, asking for the money and routine business banking—at the very least. Remember: this is a marathon not a sprint; you do not have to open the checking account right off the bat. Most banking institutions require a minimum balance to avoid banking fees. The decision to open a checking account is not one to take lightly. Bounced checks are not good and they are expensive, so be careful. Make sure your child is mature enough before you jump from a savings account to a checking account. A savings account will work just fine. You know what else is really fun? When you are a business banker (which your little munchkin will be), you get to use the special business banking line. Watch your kids eyes light up when they walk to the often *shorter* business banking line.

At age 10, Jack was too young for a checking account, so he used his savings account and it worked out fine. Make sure you work in your kids' developmental sphere. Do not ask them to do things beyond their ability and then get mad at them because you have asked for too much. If you grow the business commensurate with their developmental level and ability; neither of you will be frustrated or unhappy. This should be a positive experience for both of you.

*Slow and steady wins the race!*

---

31   Jump$tart Coalition for Personal Financial Literacy, *Annual Report*, (Washington, DC: Jump$tart Coalition for Personal Financial Literacy, 2009)
     Ben S. Bernanke, *The Importance of Financial Education and the National Jump$tart Coalition Survey*, (Washington, DC: Jump$tart Coalition for Personal Financial Literacy, 2008)

## *Business Skill #3: Execution*

Teaching our kids the value of a job well done is good; teaching them to go beyond their customers' expectations is even better. Jack is very conscientious about how he puts the cans out.

This attention to detail he has acquired since he started his business is a quality I would not change for the world. He makes sure they are *just right*. If I am helping him and I put the cans out incorrectly, he corrects them— then corrects me. Does it matter to the guy who drives the garbage truck? It probably does not, but it matters to Jack, and that makes me happy. Jack is working as if it *does* matter. When this skill is applied to something else, he will be equally as aware of the quality of the job he does.

Since Jack's business is not overly complicated, I often engage him in conversations about other businesses we frequent. We talk about a number of aspects of any given business including product quality, delivery and customer service. If I cannot create a hands-on learning experience for Jack, I will open up an opportunity with a conversation.

For example, when Jack was about five years old, he decided he wanted to be a chef. This led to him doing critiques on all the restaurants we frequented. He developed a system in which he rated the food, the service and even the ambiance. I thought it was a great way to encourage his observational skills.

We would talk about the place and he would make stars on a piece of paper. They were stars he was giving the chef. Sometimes, if we had a particularly wonderful meal, we would ask to see the chef. Jack would explain his rating system and tell the chef what "Jack Rating" the chef had earned that night.

Most of them were very good-natured about it; some were stunned; others were—as you might have guessed—not so impressed. It did not really matter because—to me—Jack was using his powers of observation. He was trying new dishes just so he could rate them; he was learning how to talk with an adult. He was engaging a stranger without Stranger Danger.

Jack's rating system created a learning opportunity for Jack and it was fun. Now, we simply observe people in action. Jack sees things without me even having to say anything. He has become very observant about customer service.

## Business Skill #4: Customer Service

The executives in The Aspen Institute and Booz Allen Hamilton Inc. research survey,[32] as discussed earlier in this chapter, said the second most important company value was customer service. Customer service was a hallmark value to those executives because commitment to their customers and the services they provide is what keeps their customers coming back.

| Commitment to Customers | North America: 87% Europe: 90% Asia/Pacific: 86% |
| --- | --- |

*Source: The Aspen Institute and Booz Allen Hamilton*

The best marketing is word of mouth. Excellent customer service gets people talking about you and your business to their friends. Good customer service is what gets your word-of-mouth business up and running.

Where kids are concerned, this is as simple as going the extra mile to take someone's newspaper to their door or front porch. The little things will get noticed because, frankly, most kids do not interact with adults on

32   Note 30, supra.

this level. It is sad to say but we often see the other side of kids. When adults meet a child who reaches out and goes the extra mile, it is unusual and something people will notice. Your kid's customer service skills will get people talking.

If you teach your child to come from a place of giving, customer service will become second nature. Teach them to under promise and over deliver; but, if they do promise, they must deliver.

In Chapter 3, I told you the story about how one week Jack and his dad forgot to do his cans. Jack took that very seriously and to heart. It was a difficult but good lesson for him regarding commitments and customer service. Your kid's customers will be very understanding, but do not let their understanding nature get in the way of the lessons you are teaching. You do not need to be hard-nosed about it, but it is not acceptable for someone to tell your kid it is okay to let a promise go unfulfilled. I'll use an example to explain what I mean. When Jack's customer heard the reason Jack had not put his cans back he said, "That's OK."

While I appreciated his kind understanding towards Jack, his leniency was sending the wrong message. Yes, it was sending understanding, but the primary lesson here was responsibility. I gently explained to his customer his graciousness was appreciated, but Jack needed to learn responsibility. As soon as the words left my mouth, I could see the understanding come across his customer's face. This is one of the cool things about working with your neighbors. They understand the lessons you are trying to teach your kids; they know they are ultimately helping you. There are many times when unspoken acknowledgement passes between one of Jack's customers and me. They *get* what I am doing, they love being a part of it and I love having them as one of my partners in crime!

Our kids need to "Work It" and "Own It"! Money does not fall out of the sky—even for millionaires. They take action, work smart and work hard. They are dedicated and driven. Teach your kids to be dedicated and driven, and they will always take the action required to be a success—no matter what they choose to do in life.

If our kids can learn early to treat their customers as a gift, they will come from a place of service. Approaching your customers from a place of service will create an atmosphere of giving. Giving is contagious. If you do this, you will find people appreciate your service more and are willing to give more in return.

## Business Skill #5: Follow-up

Your kid will learn to ask for feedback, referrals and additional ancillary opportunities as they follow up with their customers. This is the place where their business can really experience growth and expansion; it is one of the opportunities where you can teach them the art of asking.

Jack and I were recently on our way to our mountain home in Cassel, California. It is about a five hour drive from our San Jose home, so there is a lot of driving time. I am a big proponent of using driving time to learn new things. On the way, we were listening to Jack Canfield and Mark Victor Hansen's *Aladdin Factor* CD. It was not the first time I had listened to it, but it was for Jack. He really likes this stuff. Your kids will too if you introduce it to them.

We stopped outside of Sacramento to pick up two beds we needed for the house. We bought the beds from a mom and her son; we met at their storage unit to get the beds.

We loaded up the beds and, as I was getting into the car, it dawned on me maybe they were cleaning out the storage unit. I had seen stereo speakers and thought, "I bet they want to sell those speakers."

As I was getting back in the car and about to fire up the engine, I thought, "Ann, you have just been listening to Jack Canfield and Mark Victor Hansen say, "*Just ask!*"

Then I thought, "No, it is none of my business."

But, Mr. Canfield was still in my ear saying, "*Oh, what the heck ... go for it anyway!*"

I got out of the car, went back and said, "By the way, are you emptying out that storage unit?"

The son said, "Yes, I am."

"I noticed you have stereo speakers. Are you interested in selling them?"

"Yes, I am—as a matter of fact!"

"Okay then. I'll buy them!"

We needed this transaction: the son getting one more thing out of his storage unit and me getting one more thing I needed for the house. It was great and I had to laugh. Had I not been listening to those CDs, I would never have asked!

When I got back in the car, I told Jack what had happened. We could not stop laughing about it and when we unpacked the speakers—three hours later—we laughed about it again!

That experience was wonderful on many levels, but one of the things it showed *my* Jack was even his mom can learn something new. It is so important we show our kids we are lifetime learners. I learn something new every day. Every new person I meet, who has taken the time to talk, has told me some interesting story or fact. Everyone has lessons to teach and everyone has lessons to learn. Teaching our kids to absorb, learn and grow each day is a special gift; without a doubt the best way for them to receive this gift is by watching you.

Help your kids follow up with their customers by asking how they can serve them better. If you do this, your kids will be well on their way to mastering the sixth millionaire skill: "Give It".

# Just say no to allowance

Do you give your kids allowance? I have one word for you: Stop.

Most parents give their kids allowance for doing chores around the house. Chores are part of a person's obligation to their family. I don't get paid to do the dishes. I don't get paid to cook our meals. Kids need to have chores around the house as part of their family obligation.

If your kids want money, do what I do. Jack knows if he needs extra cash, he has a standing offer: he can wash my car for 10 bucks anytime! He knows if he wants additional funds, he can ask what special job he can do around the house to earn cash.

If there is something at the store your kids want you to buy, negotiate what they can do around the house to earn the privilege of the purchase. This works especially well on larger items. Set a goal together and determine how you are going to achieve the goal as a family. Maybe it is a garage sale, maybe it is a bake sale, who knows, get creative. Remove phrases like, "we can't afford that." from your vocabulary and replace them with phrases like, "what can we do to earn the money for that?"

When we were going to buy our Ford Mustang, Jack wanted to know how he could help. He wanted to contribute. It happened to be the middle of summer so I helped him make lemonade; Jack sold it and presented me with the proceeds of his sale. The money went towards the Mustang and he felt invested in the family purchase. It was fulfilling for him and it helped to show him how we can achieve anything if we work together.

I know this might sound self serving—after all, a major portion of this book is dedicated to helping kids start their own business—but I can't stress the point enough. If your kids want a regular influx of cash, help them start their own business. You will be teaching them a skill that will serve them for the rest of their life.

*Chapter 6*

# Things to Keep in Mind Before You Start the Plan

Remember, as you embark on this amazing journey; keep the end goal in mind. You are teaching your kids how to be an entrepreneur—not how to do a job. Having the millionaire skills you are teaching them will differentiate your child. They will have the skills they need to imagine the life of their dreams and the ability and belief system to achieve those dreams. If you keep the end goal in mind, you'll see opportunity after opportunity to reinforce what you are teaching them. Don't be afraid to call them on the carpet when they need it.

You are their cheerleader and their conscience all rolled into one.

Here is a recap of what you can do to help your kid with their business:

- In front of your kids, tell others how they have started their own business. Show your kids you are proud enough to brag.
- Practice their sales pitch with them and encourage them to practice it. Let them stumble a little, but do not let them fall flat on their face. Be there to support them—avoid jumping in—remember to prop them up.
- Start the business by the age of 12, if you can.
- Help your child open a savings account.
- Make sure the business grows with their developmental ability. Remember: As they age, they will get faster at the work itself, so the number of customers will have an exponential—instead of linear—growth. Here are some guidelines:

| | |
|---|---|
| 7–9 years old | Limited number of customers to maximum 20 minutes of work per workday (Jack's Garbage Valet = 5 customers) |
| 10–11 years old | Move up to 20–30 minutes per workday (Jack's Garbage Valet = 7 customers) |
| 12–13 years old | Add additional customers to a maximum of 40 minutes per workday (Jack's Garbage Valet = 10 customers) |
| 14–15 years old | Add additional customers to a maximum of 50 minutes per workday (Jack's Garbage Valet = 15–20 customers) |
| 16–18 years old | Can manage 60 minutes or more per workday (Jack's Garbage Valet = 20–30 customers) |

- Be mindful of the developmental age of your child and do not set them up to fail. This is supposed to be a positive learning experience. Make sure the method is reinforcing the madness, not just making them mad!
- If you are in a work meeting or at a movie; you turn your cell phone off. Show your kids they are just as important to you as a movie!

When you are spending time with them turn your phone off and tell them you are doing it! Be present!

- You are the support staff in your kid's business. Guide them, but let them run the show.
- You are working with your kids at the magical age when they still believe you know something! This is the time to lay the foundation to become their Trusted Advisor.
- Listen to learn! Listen to them and pause before you answer. Before you answer anything, ask yourself a couple of questions and HALT:

| Are you **Hungry?** |
| --- |
| Are you **Angry?** |
| Are you **Late?** |
| Are you **Tired?** |

I know this sounds nuts but, if you answer "Yes" to any of the HALT questions, do everything you can to put those feelings aside when you are dealing with your kids. It is natural to lose it every now and then, after all no one ever told us raising a kid would be easy. They also kept exactly how hard it would be a secret! I try to keep the HALT questions in mind when I am about to blow. Am I perfect? Nope, but I try. Thinking about and remembering HALT has helped me.

- When your kid comes to you with a struggle or a problem, transition yourself from parent to Trusted Advisor by using these four questions:

  1. **What do you want?** This is the most important question. This is where you are *listening to learn*. Using reflective listening skills; parrot back to them what you heard. You do this for two reasons. Firstly, you want to make sure you heard them correctly. Secondly, you want to help them clarify and understand exactly what they want. What is the final outcome they are seeking?

  2. **What are you doing to get it?** (Note: "*it*" refers to "what your child wants".) This question helps your child look at what they are doing. Are they part of the problem or the solution? Is what they are doing contributing to the problem? You are gently— *gently*—exploring their current actions at this step.

3. **Is it working?** This question helps to shed light on the status of their current efforts. Is what they are currently doing to fix the problem working? Truth is, the chances are if it was working they would not be coming to you, so the expected answer here is "No".

4. **Do you want to figure out another way?** Can I help you figure out another way? These questions are asked more as a way of getting permission for you to offer a solution. Before they will listen to your suggestions, they have to want to hear them.

Walk them through these questions and you will be surprised how they might have a new solution to the problem or at least something to try. You are not telling them what to do but instead helping them come up with a solution. You are working on it together. Approach this exchange from a place of service. You are trying to help—not dictate. You are the Trusted Advisor. In addition, at the next opportunity, do not forget to ask them if the new solution worked!

# Friends vs. Friendly

I think one of the hardest lessons to teach our kids is being gracious. The truth is, not everyone we meet is going to like us, be our friend or want to spend time with us. You know what? That is OK. It is OK if I am not every one's cup of tea. What is not OK is treating someone poorly. We need to be gracious with everyone—regardless of how we believe they feel about us or how we feel about them. What do I mean by gracious? I mean being polite and treating everyone with tact and kindness.

In our house, we have a saying; "You don't have to be everyone's friend, but you do have to be friendly." There is simply no reason to treat people badly. We have to remember, kids can easily misinterpret how someone is behaving and assume the person doesn't like them. Our kids are still maturing and it is easy to make an innocent mistake.

continued on next page...

...continued from previous page

At my age, I can still make a mistake and think the worst. If we are right and the person does not like us, it is not likely we are going to kill them with kindness and change their opinion; that is not the point. The point is; it is beneath us to behave any other way.

This is a hard concept for kids to understand. After all, each of us feels the need to be liked. We all get our feelings hurt when someone behaves as if they don't like us. It is a natural reaction to behave indifferent or badly towards someone that we think dislikes us. This is why it is important to teach this specific lesson to our kids. In doing so, we can help them overcome a natural urge and teach them a more mature behavior.

I think our motto is a great way to explain one of the hardest and often most hurtful lessons in life. Not everyone wants to, has to or needs to be my friend, and the way I think they feel about me won't stop me from being friendly.

Remember: our kids are growing up. They are in middle childhood and need to understand why things happen so they can properly process them. They also have a growing need for some control over what is happening. When they were little, we could direct their behavior by telling them, "Do this" or "Do that". Now, they are too grown up for that proscriptive kind of dictatorship. Set up a framework that will make you happy and them a part of the process. At this point in their development, when you have a conflict about something that is non-negotiable, you can still use a proscriptive approach but try these statements to help you get your point across in a respectful but firm manner:

1. **This is what I want.** Tell them exactly what you want to have happen.
2. **This is what I understand you are doing.** Explain to them what your perception is of what they are doing.
3. **This is why that isn't working for me.** Explain why what they are doing is not acceptable.
4. **Here is what I need you to do.** Tell them exactly what you want them to do. Be specific.
5. **Can I count on you to help me by doing this the way I need it done?** This is where you respectfully get them to buy into your request.

When we use a proscriptive approach to conflict resolution with our kids, we show them we respect them as thinking people. It usually results in an immediate change of behavior because we are clear about exactly what we want them to do. We take the guesswork out of it. It also gives us a chance to explain the basis for our request. I am not saying you need to explain yourself to your kids.

I am saying it is helpful to explain your thought process. They can better understand and accept your decision when they know the thought process behind your decision. Your explanation also teaches them how to think things through; you are verbally demonstrating your thought process. This kind of exchange is a healthier interaction and gives you a better chance to move forward with a more cooperative approach.

## Don't say "Don't!"

> "If all our kids ever hear is don't, when it comes to
> their dreams they won't."
>
> —Ann Morgan James

Ever been in a really crowded room—you can barely hear yourself think—and all of a sudden from across the room you hear your kid calling your name? It has always amazed me how my brain can suddenly focus in on the important sounds—like my name—out of all the other noise. Turns out to be nothing magical, it is a part of our brain called the reticular activating system, which makes that sort of thing possible.

The reticular activating system is an automatic mechanism at the base of our brains that delivers relevant information to our attention. It basically acts as the gatekeeper between our conscious and our subconscious brain. Think of it as a filter between your conscious mind and your subconscious mind. It brings to the forefront those things it deems to be important, like your kid calling your name in a crowded room.

To be completely scientific and exact, the reticular activating system connects the brain stem—the lower part of the brain—to the cerebral cortex through various neural pathways. It acts as the bridge between the lower and upper part of the brain. Why is this significant? It connects the part of the brain that controls reflexes and involuntary functions to the place in the brain where consciousness and thinking abilities live. Amongst other things, the reticular activating system is responsible for our survival instincts. In short the reticular activating system has a deep relationship with the awareness functions of our brain.

Great science lesson Ann, but why is this important to my kid? Good question. It is important because—like any filter—the reticular activating system does not always filter out everything. For example, it cannot filter out certain words like don't, won't or can't. It only hears, receives and filters what it thinks we need to hear. Our subconscious mind can't process a negative so it tosses out the negative words. I'll give you an example: right now, I *don't* want you to think about a giraffe.

How many of you, if even for a split second saw a giraffe in your mind's eye? That is because you are reading something, and your reticular activating system knows it is important, so it brings the information in, but it can't process the word "don't".

Have you ever told your kid, "don't spill that glass of milk" only to find the next thing you know, the milk is on the floor? Their brain heard "spill the milk" and it did what you wanted it to do. As parents, we need to change the way we talk with our kids and ourselves. Remove words like "don't" from your vocabulary and approach everything from the positive. Here is an example of what I am talking about. Instead of saying, "Don't blow your test today", try "I know you studied hard for your test, I just know you are going to do a fantastic job!"

What I am talking about here is very profound. I am talking about changing your children's beliefs about themselves. What is a belief? It is the acceptance of something being true. *Merriam-Webster* says a belief is a "conviction of the truth of some statement or the reality of some being or phenomenon especially when based on examination of evidence."[33] Beliefs start somewhere. They start as ideas. Whether it is an idea put in our kid's head by us, their teachers, other kids or other adults; it does not matter. The idea is put in our kid's head and their reticular activating system filters in data to prove the theory. Did you hear that? Our brains filter *in* information to prove an idea. So follow me: if our kids get the idea in their heads they are stupid, their brain is going to grab onto every incident to prove that idea is correct. Once your mind has enough references for the idea, it becomes a *belief*. This is how an idea becomes a belief and exactly why beliefs are hard to change.

This is why it was such an uphill climb for me to change Jack's perception of himself. He had heard from the bullies at school he was dumb. He had gotten outside information because of his struggles with Dyslexia which made him feel stupid. His self-esteem was at an all time low when I got him to start his business. Slowly, each win contradicted the beliefs he had formed about himself. Inch by inch, we climbed out of the hole his beliefs had helped him dig for himself. Once I realized what was going on, once I educated myself, I worked double time to turn those beliefs around for Jack. Helping him become an entrepreneur was a huge step in the right direction because outside information—his customers and other adults—reinforced

my assertions that he was worthy, bright and a great kid.

When Jack and I catch each other using *don't* or *can't* or *won't*, we correct ourselves and each other and we exercise our "Believe It" millionaire skill daily! We can poke fun at ourselves when we catch ourselves using a negative. We tease each other and laugh together about it.

Why the giraffe? I have collected giraffes since I was 16 years old. I have

33    Merriam-Webster Online Dictionary, Springfield, MA 2011 by Merriam-Webster, Incorporated

always loved them because when things are just out of reach—they stretch. They stretch to eat and drink. Giraffes have always been a metaphor for my life. With Dyslexia, I had to stretch to get through school. I had to stretch to finish college. I had to stretch to start my business. When I started educating myself about how to help Jack and came upon the reticular activating system, I loved that it was *reticular*. After all, I love reticulated giraffes. There have been many times over the past few years when I felt I was taking two steps back for each step forward in my quest to help Jack regain his self-esteem. When those setbacks felt like they would overwhelm me, I remembered my giraffe—and stretched.

## *Pushin' the positive every chance I get*

> *"A good listener is not only popular everywhere, but after a while he knows something."*
>
> —*Wilson Mizner*

Affirmations are positive ideas you can plant in your brain. Once you put an affirmation seed in the brain, the reticular activating system will begin working to find supporting evidence or references to prove your idea to be true. We can literally reprogram our brains to accept a new belief. If your kid is stuck with the notion he or she is stupid, you can change that belief by putting a new idea into the reticular activating system. The easiest way to put the new idea into the system is through affirmations.

After getting Jack to start his business, I knew I needed to do more to really get his self-esteem running at full throttle. I started using affirmations to help bring the "Believe It" millionaire skill to life. We started a ritual of creating positive affirmations to start our day. I talked about these in a parenting pearl called Popsicle® Pros, but it is worth a second mention. Each morning we drive to school, we think of the affirmation we want for the day. Remember, it is critical that you do this *with* your kid. They need to see affirmations are not just hocus-pocus you are making them do; they need to see it is something you do too. The affirmations can be simple; Jack's first one was, "I am happy."

The important parts are:

- They should start with I am.
- They need to be short and concise.
- They are better with action verbs.
- They need an emotional connect.
- They should have a timeframe.

Here are three of mine:

- I am happily enjoying my size 10 clothes on my vacation in June.
- I am calmly interacting with my amazing son Jack every day.
- I am productively marking items off today's Ta-Da List.

Here are three of Jack's:

- I am happily one of the NY Times best-selling authors for the month of May.
- I am a focused student today.
- I am happily getting an A on my spelling test today.

These affirmations have become an important part of our morning ritual. We also have 3x5 inch cards on our mirrors in our bathrooms—with other affirmations—which we see and say each day. We are effectively planting new beliefs for our reticular activating systems to chew on and it feels great. Yep, this old dog had some new tricks to learn. Doing this activity with Jack was been one more step in the journey to Trusted Advisor.

I have come across so many parenting resources, it is almost overwhelming. I have pulled together a page that gives you some of the ones I like the most.

Much like the other pages, there is a little something for everyone. Be sure to take a look, I think you'll find some interesting tips there.

One of my favorites is about Parents and Dating—you dating, not the kids dating silly!

**www.howtoraiseamillionaire.com/ parenting**

*Chapter 7*

# Five Days from Ordinary to Extraordinary

*"All our dreams can come true, if we have the courage to pursue them."*

—*Walt Disney*

This chapter—divided into days—will outline the required tasks to start your kid's business. The days do not have to be consecutive; you can do the tasks once a week, over a month's time or combine the tasks and make it a one-day activity. The speed with which you help your child start their business is entirely up to you! Do what works for your kid, your family and you.

## What Is Your Timeframe?

When Jack said, "Yes, I'll do it", I had to go for it right then and there; so we did it quickly and were up and running in a week. The timeframe of this venture depends on your goals; how much time you both want to devote to starting the business and your child's capabilities. You have one shot at this. Pushing too hard—making it a chore instead of something cool you do together—will ruin it. Think of where your child is developmentally and plan accordingly. If they are dying to get started; then go for it! If you feel little doses would work better; then take it one day at a time. You know your child best.

If you are a person who does not want to reinvent the wheel, has never started your own business, wants to get a fast start or just wants a little guidance to make it easier, our Fast Start Action Guide is the kit for you. The Fast Start Action Guide includes:

- Step-by-step instructions
- Fill-in-the-blank action planning sheet
- Flyer templates
- Invoice forms
- Accounting tally sheets

You can find it at howtoraiseamillionaire.com.

## Day #1: Time to Pick a Horse

### What Kind of Business?

The first thing to do is help your child determine what kind of business to start. This activity should take about 1 hour.

Like any good project, the idea of helping your kid start a business needs a little planning—reverse engineering—if you will.

They might have great ideas about what business to start or no clue at all. Your job is to think of the bigger picture, see the options from all sides and guide—not dictate—your kid. If you help them understand and learn how to evaluate any situation, you'll be giving them the gift of objectivity and teaching them evaluation techniques; which are both important life skills.

Open a dialog and explore all the options with them. You are going to be the devil's advocate, but remember: nobody likes a naysayer. Do not be negative about their ideas. Avoid the "I don't think ...." and "That's not a good idea ..." sentences. Part of this exercise is to get their creative juices going, and you do not want to squash the process.

**How Long Will It Take?**

Every business takes time and you need to keep this in mind when your kid is evaluating which business to start. It is your responsibility to understand how the business will fit into their existing schedule and what it will take to get it done.

# The Parking Lot

The Parking Lot technique, used in corporate meetings, keeps conversations on track but does not stop the creative flow of ideas.

Here how it works: keep a piece of paper handy and label it Parking Lot. If your kid brings up a subject which is off the course of the current conversation or promises to distract or disrupt what you are doing, write it on the paper and go back to the task or conversation at hand. Once you finish what you are doing, go back and devote your full attention to the subject your kid wanted to explore. If it works into what you are doing, great; if it is just something that came into your kid's mind and they wanted to talk about it, that is fine, too.

It demonstrates that our kid's thoughts are valid and shows you think they have something important to tell you. It also teaches them a thought—at any given moment—may not be the right conversation for that moment. They learn to "hold the thought" until the time is right.

It gives both of you a way to remember what they were going to say but still keep the current conversation on track. This is a great tool to use during homework when distractions mean extra time.

If you think something will take half an hour, add 15 minutes for a "fudge factor." Tasks often take more time than you think, and you will need to make sure the job is doable. For example, there have been times when I help Jack put cans out or pull cans in because we are in a time crunch. We have developed a routine, which makes it easier; the routine reduces the stress of doing the business. Give yourself a break when you are developing your routine because it takes time to get in the groove. Write yourself notes or do whatever helps you add this new routine into the mix. Don't forget, you are the positive one here. If there are challenges in the beginning, you are the one who is going to be the cheerleader and talk about how you can do this together!

## What Is the Big Picture?

Jack was reluctant to build a business around things he did not like doing. I did not anticipate this one and it surprised me. At first, he only looked at the task—he would be taking the garbage out—and not at the fact people were paying him to do it and he was going to get money.

This was hard for me to understand. I made my living doing events. When I am at an event for my clients, it is my job to make sure the appearance of the event is pristine. If I am walking around and see garbage on the floor or a dirty glass on a table, I pick up the garbage and take the dirty glass away. No, it is not my job, and yes, I hire people to do those tasks, but it is my job to look at the big picture—the end game. If my end goal is to have a happy client and dirty dishes make the event look sloppy, I am not above pitching in to help get to the finish line. I had to teach Jack *that* kind of thinking and it was not easy. If you smell a teaching moment, you are right.

There are times in life when the almighty dollar is the thing you need. I helped Jack understand the measure of a successful businessman is a happy customer—not "the job". Taking the garbage out is just taking the garbage out. To steal an old saying from KNBR personality Ron Lyons, "That would be like putting lipstick on a pig."[34] Taking garbage cans out is just not glamorous—no matter how you push the can.

When your kids balk at the job itself—whatever it is—remind them they are performing a service for their neighbors. They found a need and they are filling it. If all else fails, remind them they are also in it for *the money!*☺

"Think of all the action figures you can buy just by dragging someone's garbage cans to the street, Jack. When you are doing it, just say to yourself, 'This one's for Captain Rex.' 'This one's for Obi Wan.' 'For Yoda, this one is!'"

## *Four Easy Steps:*

To help you guide the conversation in determining the best business idea to fit your kid, your family and your lifestyle, follow these four easy steps:

**Step #1: Brainstorming Possible Businesses**

With your kid, take out a piece of paper and write down your ideas with a brief description of the business. Our Fast Start Action Guide has a rule: Parents do all the writing. This is not supposed to be homework. Making them write makes it like homework. You do the writing. It will go faster, you'll have an active part in the process and it will make everyone happier. This is a dialog and a brainstorming session. Make a list and evaluate it. Do not eliminate any ideas. Even if you think it is the goofiest idea in the world, do not toss it out—write it down. Besides, the goofy ideas provide a good laughing moment! Let the evaluation process sift through the list. The process will naturally make the good ideas bubble up to the surface; the bad ideas might make a good ancillary income. The evaluation process will allow plenty of time to review each idea logically. Your kid will conclude what is a good idea and what is a bad one.

---

34 Jay Mathews, *San Francisco Tries To Keep Baseball Raiders at Bay*, (Washington, DC: The Washington Post, November 1985)

## Step #2: Identify the Important Criteria

Once you have the list, decide on important criteria and put it across the top of the paper. You are making a table so you can talk through each business idea. Use your preplanning skills and help guide the conversation to include those areas that are important to you. For example, if your family goes dirt bike riding each weekend, a business requiring weekend work is not an option. You are not there to squelch creativity. Let your kids think of as many ideas as they can. By thinking of all the areas of importance, such as weekday work or no driving required, and putting the criteria on the list, you are asserting they have value.

Here is a sample table we used for discussion about Jack's business:

| Business Idea | Can Start Tomorrow | No Driving Required | Steady Income | Not on Weekends |
|---|---|---|---|---|
| Garbage Valet | X | X | X | X |
| Babysitting | Training Required | X | | |
| Pet Sitting | X | X | | |
| Vacation Mail | X | X | | |
| Jedi Warrior | X | | | |

I wanted Jack to start a Garbage Valet business, but we had a number of other options as well. This type of table can show your kid the best option for the primary business they should start. The other businesses can be optional services your kid can offer to their neighbors. They can become ancillary sources of income to make your kid's business even stronger.

## Step #3: Determine Value Proposition

Evaluate each business option and teach them to determine the value proposition. The more value a business has, the higher the value proposition. Open the dialog on each business option. Rate each option based on the criteria you selected in Step #2. If you do not have your criteria, this step will not work well. Keep in mind, in this process you might both come up with additional criteria that are important to you and your family, so add them to the list. Once you start to evaluate things based on your criteria, the winners will naturally bubble up to the top.

**Step #4: Make Your Decision**

Together, decide what business your kid is going to start. It might or might not be the one you thought of in the first place. Remember you can somewhat drive the conversation with your criteria selection. Remember, you are the adult and knowledge is power—do not abuse it! If there is something you want your kid to do, but you know they oppose it, do not abuse the tactic and force them into something they will hate. A successful person loves what they do, so boxing your kid into a corner will only backfire in the end. You can't force the "Love It" millionaire skill, so be mindful of your influence.

## Day #2: Set Up Your Marketing

*"When you believe in a thing, believe in it all the way, implicitly and unquestionable."*

—*Walt Disney*

**Tips for Making a Flyer**

It is now time to make a flyer, and here are some tips:

- Keep it simple.
- Make it fun.
- Show the benefits of using your service.
- Design an eye-catching headline. Pictures are fun and can help get the point across.
- Do not overload the page with too much to read.
- Focus on benefits.
- Include contact information.
- Use no more than three different fonts. This includes size, font and font style.

Here are some tricks we used in Jack's first flyer:

1. We used humor and something people could identify with to catch their attention.
2. We used reversed-out text (white text on a black background).
3. We printed on brightly colored paper with black ink to keep the cost down.
4. We used Jack's logo to get recognition. (Our Fast Start Action Guide includes a custom designed logo for your business!)

---

**EVER PANIC BECAUSE YOU FORGOT TO PUT THE CANS OUT AND YOU CAN HEAR THE TRUCK RUMBLE BY?**

**TIRED OF HAULING THOSE GARBAGE CANS TO THE CURB?**

INTRODUCING A NEW NEIGHBORHOOD SERVICE...

# Jack's

# Garbage

# Valet

DON'T WORRY ANYMORE!
HIRE ME, YOUR NEIGHBOR JACK JAMES!

FOR JUST $5 A MONTH YOU CAN STOP WORRYING ABOUT YOUR GARBAGE CANS.

I'LL TAKE YOUR CANS OUT AND IN FOR YOU!

**SIGN-UP FOR MY SERVICE!**
**CALL: XXX-XXXX**
**EMAIL: XXXX@XXXXXXXXXXX.COM**

5.  We did not make it too busy with too many fonts. The human brain is confused if there are too many fonts. We used one font with bold and one font with regular, that makes two total.

6.  Less is more! We wrote less to make it count.

7.  We put Jack's picture on the flyer to make it more personal. After all, these folks see us around the neighborhood and—if they see him—they will recognize him.

8.  We included Jack's contact info. Note: I monitored Jack's email so I knew if he got a response.

If you do not get your first flyer quite right, you will have another shot. It does not have to perfect. Hand-written flyers made by your kid are great, too. Do what works for your family.

After we distributed his first flyer, Jack had about four customers. It was time for his next marketing and sales effort: his second flyer.

Again, we tried to be funny with the header by making the garbage can talk.

•  We put Jack's logo front and center.

•  We made it a half sheet, which cut the cost in half and used less paper. After people have seen the first flyer, they know who you are. You can do half sheets after the initial flyer.

•  We put Jack's picture on the flyer, again.

•  His contact information is obvious and not hidden.

Have fun! Make it memorable and it will stick in their minds. Proofread it carefully because typos can put people off. With my Dyslexia, I miss my own mistakes, so I try to have someone else proof my work to make sure it is correct.

## Day #3: Begin Your Sales

> *"Pretend that every single person you meet has a sign around his or her neck that says, "Make me feel important." Not only will you succeed in sales, you will succeed in life."*
>
> —*Mary Kay Ash*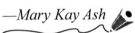

### Refine the Sales Pitch

It is now time to exercise your kid's "Asking" and "Next" muscles! Before you go out into the neighborhood, your kid should have their quick two to three sentence sales pitch ready.

As I mentioned in Chapter 2, here is Jack's sales pitch:

> "Hi! My name is Jack James. I am your neighbor and I live on XYZ Street. Are you getting tired of taking your garbage cans in and out? Then hire me! For $10 a month, I'll take your cans in and out and you won't have to worry anymore."

This did not roll right off his tongue at first; it took some time to practice it. It is important to talk about it beforehand and practice it a few times. Then, remember, I said the hardest part is to sit on your hands and not interrupt your kid when they are trying to deliver their pitch. If they get tongue-tied, remember, encourage them with a few key words to get them rolling, but do your best not to interrupt them when they are trying to get it out.

### Make Your Way through the Neighborhood

With your flyers in hand, start making your way through the neighborhood. Remember: It is against the law to put anything in a person's mailbox. They

can put it on the porch, the doorknob or have it sticking out from under the door mat. If your kid is starting a Garbage Valet like Jack, tape it on the can!

With any luck, you will run into some neighbors and your kid will get a chance to practice their pitch. Not everyone is going to jump at the wonderful service opportunity offered, but there will be some. If you think no one will go for it, make sure to "seed" the neighborhood. Pick out a couple of neighbors you know and ask them to say "Yes" if you pay for the service. You are doing this to build confidence and make sure your kid gets a customer. Only you know the landscape of your neighborhood. If your budding entrepreneur runs into barriers, encourage them to offer to do their service for a month free; if the clients like the service, they probably will continue. This strategy works very well because the first couple of times your kid does their cans for them; they will be hooked! Jack does this a lot now! It works like a charm!

### Setting Expectations

When setting expectations, remind your kid they should expect 20 "No's" before they get one "Yes". It makes it more fun if you make it a game and keep a tally. Tell them "No" means "Not today" because they might get them next time! You are building their "Asking" and "Next" muscles—muscles that will serve them for life. Keep a positive attitude and do not get discouraged or impatient. You have to take the lead here and if you do, they will follow.

Expectations should be set with your child's customer. I own a home-based business, so I can help Jack after school. However, if I worked 9 to 5, Jack would need to inform his customers he would take the cans out between 7 and 8 p.m. If Jack and I are going on vacation, and his dad cannot do his cans, we give his customers a courtesy notice; which tells them to put out their own cans. You know what happens when you *assume*: so set expectations. If something happens, it is time to apologize!

## Day #4: Set Up Accounting

> "The two most beautiful words in the English language are 'check enclosed'."
>
> —*Dorothy Parker*

**Tracking Your Work**

This step should occur between getting the first customer and the first day of implementation. Before you start the job, make sure you have a way to track the work. Do not do what we did and set this up after the fact.

When Jack got his first customer, I did not even have a way to write down her name. Not great modeling for the kid—I told you I was human! I had to keep repeating it over and over to myself to remember it. (No…I didn't have my cell phone to text it to myself either!) I make mistakes all the time! I urge you to use the system we developed and save yourself some heartache. We put together a Service Order Sheet to help keep track of who had signed up for Jack's service.

# Jack's Garbage Valet

## Service Order Sheet

Customer Name: _____

Address: _____

Phone: _____

Email: _____

I prefer for you to contact me by:

❒     Phone

❒     Email

❒     Both

I am ordering:

❒     Garbage Valet

❒     Garbage Valet with Tidy Curb

Start Date: _____

The Service Order Sheet answers all the questions you need to get started:

- The proper spelling of their name
- The best way to reach them, which is important if you are going to be on vacation and will not be there to do your service
- Exactly what service they want

Then, you can go back home and add them to your software package, your spreadsheet, or your notebook—whatever method you are using to keep track of your accounting. You can even make a notebook out of the Service Order Sheets to keep track.

## Accounting Options

My dad was a certified public accountant. When I started my first business, he handed me a ledger. (I still have it!) I recorded my invoices and the date they were paid. He gave the same lesson to my brother and I would be willing to bet, if I asked my brother, "Do you still have that ledger?" He would say, "Yes!"

As my business grew and accounting software became less expensive, I moved to a software program.

Dad was old school, and you know what? Old school works just fine. If you have no desire to involve your kid in computer software, a notebook will work. All that matters is keeping good records.

If you want to wade into the shallow end of computers, use a spreadsheet program like Excel® which is included in Microsoft Office®. OpenOffice.org, a set of open productivity tools, is free downloadable software available at openoffice.org. It works a lot like Office. I used it for years when I contracted to Sun Microsystems. If you want your kid to prepare for the real world, invest in software. It is not cheap, but it is a great way for them to learn. I have Intuit QuickBooks®.

There are plenty of free shareware accounting packages available on the Internet, such as GnuCash (www.gnucash.org), which I have never used.

Before downloading or using any free software, I suggest first you do a Google search to make sure it is legit. Read the reviews and make sure it is safe to download.

Here is a sample invoice from Jack's Garbage Valet:

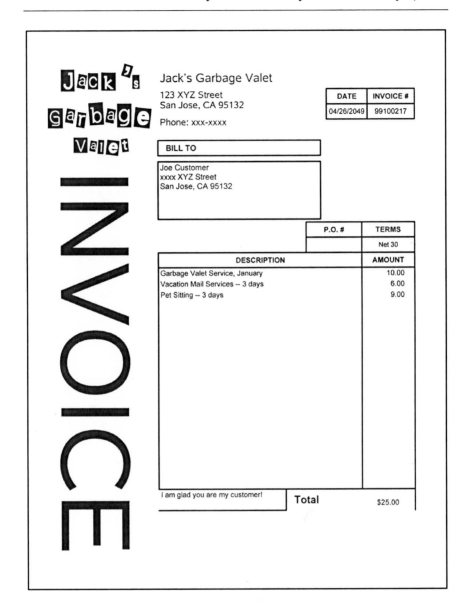

There are three ways—a hand written ledger, a spreadsheet or business accounting software—to help your kid understand and master basic accounting. It is up to you to choose the method which works for your family and situation. It is also important to teach your kids how to keep their checkbook in balance and reconcile their bank statements—both very important life skills.

## *Day #5: Execute*

> *"By giving kids an allowance, you teach that child to work for money rather than learn to create money."*
> —*Robert Kiyosaki*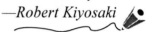

**Garbage Day Has Arrived!**

Whether it is garbage day or some other day, the day your kid starts their business is a huge day! It is a very special time and you will be proud of them. It might seem like a little thing, but it is not. It can be a turning point in your child's life. This may be the day your kid learns they can do and be anything. Be proud, happy and celebrate this victory—you *both* did it!

No matter what business your child has decided to start, the first day of implementation is important. As part of Day #1, you have thought about the organization of your child's business. At first, Jack and I thought we would be walking around our neighborhood and doing Jack's cans. That idea quickly went out the window. We live in the foothills and, while it is a great way to get exercise, walking Jack's route took a solid hour. Since we do not have that kind of time between homework and other commitments, we drive!

When I was a kid, my big brother Charlie—or Buck, as we call him—had a paper route to deliver newspapers. I remember driving around with my mom and Buck on his paper route. He will now defend to the death the fact he did most of the deliveries himself, but I remember going with them and loving it. I would watch my brother toss paper after paper onto the porches. I especially remember him throwing one down onto the driveway from Buena Vista Road to the house on Golden Gate Avenue. It was on a wicked hairpin turn. He would throw it from above and nail it every time! It was a family affair. Mom helped Buck do his route. It was time she took out of her busy schedule to help her son. My mom worked. We were latchkey kids, but she still made time for his business.

Today, Buck is a successful businessman who has owned and operated many businesses over the years. My parents' support of his businesses as a youth helped form his belief system and work ethic. I know he would agree with me when I say our parents fostered an entrepreneurial spirit in each of us, which has grown and allowed us to be successful business owners. Our parents taught us to "Dream It", "Believe It", "Love It", "Work It", "Own It" and "Give It"!

In this chapter, there are samples of Jack's flyers, his invoice and his service order form. In the book, they are rather small and hard to read.

I wanted to provide you with a page where you could get a better look at these documents and also give you some additional tips on how to create your own.

**www.howtoraiseamillionaire.com/abetterlook**

*Chapter 8*

# Some Final Thoughts

*"A life is not important except in the impact it has on other lives."*

—*Jackie Robinson*

## When I Was a Kid

When I was a kid, you went out to play with all the kids in the neighborhood. We played hide-and-go-seek until it was time for dinner; now we have to make "play dates" for our kids to hang out.

When I was a kid, if you were thirsty and you were out playing, you went over to the garden hose at your buddy's house and got a drink; now everyone has to have bottled water. Consider turning on the tap; statistics prove our water is still safe to drink.[35]

When I was a kid, if you misbehaved in public or at school, you "were in trouble". If you did not *get it* then, you knew you were going to *get it* when you got home. I am not talking about spanking. I am talking about consequences. We knew there were consequences so you just didn't misbehave.

Now, before anyone goes off the deep end and thinks I am saying anyone should beat or spank their kids to keep them in line, think again. *I am not.* I

---

35  Natural Resources Defense Council, *Bottled Water Pure Drink or Pure Hype?*, (New York, NY: Natural Resources Defense Council, 1999)
www.nrdc.org/water/drinking/bw/bwinx.asp

will, however, assert that in some cases, we have abdicated our authority over our children.

## Parental Arsenal

If you want proof of this lack of authority, look at our schools. In my experience with elementary and middle school kids, few parents think *their* little darling is at fault for anything. In many ways, we have tied the hands of our teachers. Once you move into high school, it is like a battleground of wits. There are few consequences. Kids need boundaries. Over the years, I have seen many parents have absolutely no control—much less influence—over their young kids. I cringe when I think what is in store for them when their kids are teenagers.

Do you think these kids, who roll their eyes and do not listen to their parents in elementary school, are going to suddenly pay attention and respond to their parent's authority and whims when they are in high school? Doubtful. Am I saying I am a model parent? Far from it, but I recognized early on I had to somehow command authority from Jack.

When Jack was about two or three years old, our neighbor in Cassel, Lois, gave me an incredibly straightforward and practical book by Madelyn Swift called *Discipline for Life: Getting it Right with Children*.[36] Amazon's listing describes the book quite well:

> What do you want from discipline? Better behaved, more cooperative children? Certainly! This book gives you practical, helpful techniques for accomplishing this. But don't stop there. Discipline can accomplish so much more.
>
> We also want emotionally healthy, respectful, responsible, self-disciplined children who know how to make sound decisions, communicate effectively, solve problems with skill, handle difficult situations with grace, and treat others with dignity.
>
> What we teach with our discipline at ages 2, 5, and 12, will return to help or haunt us during their adolescence and adulthood. The tips, traps, and stories found in this book help us discipline

---

36    Madelyn Swift, *Discipline for Life: Getting it Right with Children*, (Keller, TX: Childright; 2nd Revised edition, 1999)

effectively today yet keep an eye toward the future. For we will reap what we sow.[37]

In my head, I have repeatedly thanked Lois for giving me that book. Ms. Swift talks about, as she puts it, how "Mommy the Good" and "Mommy the Bad" resides in us all. Boy is she right! I have read her book multiple times.

Hey, I am human. In the heat of battle, I have not always used the best techniques and have found myself screaming at Jack like a crazy person. I admit it. I need a refresher course now and again. Ms. Swift's ideas and techniques are great, and the best part is you see results.

Part of her philosophy is to help you teach your children the power of choice and to teach there are consequences to all choices we make in life. We empower our kids when they understand the way they behave in a given situation is a *choice*—one *they* make—and those choices can have good or bad consequences.

The notion of bribery or rewards should not be in your parental arsenal. There is no "If you do *this*, I'll give you *that*." Ms. Swift teaches when you use bribes with your kids, the bribes just get bigger as the kids get older. Bribes do not exist around every corner in the real world, and we have to teach our children how to function in the real world. We need to arm them with critical

---

37   Amazon URL www.amazon.com/Discipline-Life-Getting-Right-Children/dp/1887069062

thinking skills and set them up to approach life by making sound and thoughtful decisions about their behavior and reactions to what life throws at them.

She said *parental arsenal*. That is right, folks ... we are in a battle here. If you think we are not, you are putting your head in the sand.

- Have you been in line at the grocery store and heard a fellow shopper speak to a store employee as if he or she were beneath them?
- Have you been on the receiving end of a young person at their job whose training did not include respecting their customer?
- Have you met anyone who behaves as if they are entitled and who thinks it is necessary to say everything and anything that comes to their mind—out loud?
- Have you watched a television show—cable or network—with characters using smart-aleck overtones?

*Merriam-Webster* defines "smart aleck" as "an obnoxiously conceited and self-assertive person with pretensions to smartness or cleverness."[38]

Jack and I like to watch a certain television show. I will not name it, but one of the main characters is a girl in high school. I cannot think of one episode where she is not using cutting remarks and putting down the others on the show. It is astonishing how downright *mean* her comments are to her family members. Do people laugh? Yep. But, she is making jokes at the others' expense.

I am purposely not telling you the name of the show or the network. I bet 25% or less would correctly guess the show's name. What does that tell me? It illustrates how many shows our kids are watching with behavior that should not be acceptable.

What does it really mean? It means our kids are bombarded with bad behavior from all sides and it is our responsibility as parents to point out the bad behavior to them.

Yes, every generation has their shows with comic relief that is not "nice." I am not Pollyanna; however, if you want to raise a kid who is polite and respects others, you had better monitor what your kids are watching.

When I was growing up, our parents did not allow us to watch television in the afternoon. Guess what? Neither is Jack. A few hours in the evening

---

38   Merriam-Webster URL: www.merriam-webster.com/dictionary/smart%20aleck

were acceptable. On top of that, Mom forbade us to watch *The Three Stooges* because of the violence. She set a boundary in her home. She felt the level of violence in *The Three Stooges* too excessive and she didn't want her kids watching it. Excessive or not, she had boundaries.

I am not opposed to my son watching television; I am a realist who knows television is part of our culture. I am suggesting we watch it *with* our kids and open a dialog about what we are watching. Jack and I talk about it all the time. I often remind him it might be funny to watch and laugh but, in real life, what the character is saying would be very hurtful and wrong.

## *The Power of Consequence*

Back to the battle. Here is my firsthand experience with the power of consequence.

I was having trouble with Jack because he was starting to talk back. After all, he was reaching puberty! Repeated requests to stop—at times accompanied by yelling and indignation—did not work. It was time for action.

I went back to Ms. Swift's book—*the* book—which reminded me I had not set up any consequence for his behavior choice. I knew I had to hit him where it hurt the most: *Star Wars the Clone Wars* action figures! (Thanks again, George Lucas.)

The next time he mouthed off, I was ready.

"Jack, you have a choice. You can either decide to speak to me with respect or the next time you talk back to me—just one word—you will lose one of your *Star Wars* guys for a week."

Have you ever been with your parents as an "adult child" (a term my mother's doctor always used to describe me) and you take a walk down memory lane and say something like, "I remember when I was little, Mom, and you used to make me eat all my vegetables before I could leave the table!"?

Well, when *I* am old and gray, and Jack and *his* family are over for a visit, I guarantee I will hear something like, "When I was little, Mom, and you started a sentence with, 'Jack, you have a choice…,' I *knew* I was not going to like the end of *that* sentence!"

I think Ms. Swift would be proud.

It did not take long before the first *Star Wars* clone had to march into quarantine. I had to think of some place to put the little guy so it could serve as a constant reminder. One clone gone among a zillion does not impact any given *Star Wars* battle on any given day. However, I was selective about my captives and knew Captain Rex was Jack's *fav*. Captain R. was a marked man!

I decided to hang my captives upside down by one foot in the dining room window. Before long, I had a whole squad of men hanging in my window. Okay, so this bad habit was a little harder to break than most. It still rears its ugly head on occasion and the boys go back in the window!

One night, we had a Cub Scout den meeting. The boys came over to our house and I had forgotten to take down Jack's *Star Wars* men. When the boys saw them, they had several questions about why Captain Rex and the men were dangling from the window upside-down. I waited until all the boys arrived because it made no sense in repeating the story seven times.

I explained Jack's choice. He could either speak to me with respect or he could mouth off and one of his clones would hang in the window. As we went around the room, I asked each boy to tell me about the consequences in his house. Admittedly, it was not a proper sampling—with a statistical model of plus or minus 5% scientific degree of certainty—but it was good enough for me. Half the boys had real consequences in their homes; half did not. One boy said nothing, accompanied by the obligatory shoulder shrug.

My conclusion: not enough parents have concrete consequences for their kids. I often ask myself why. My guess—again unscientific—it takes a lot of effort. You have to be consistent, stick to your guns, follow through or they will figure out your threats of consequences are hollow. The fact is, consequences work and are worth the effort.

## The Delicate Dance: When should their voice be heard?

There comes a time in every parent's life when your kid puts you into a situation where you wish you could crawl out on all fours. Mine came one day when Jack and I went to the archery store. I was teaching class at Cub Camp and I needed supplies for my campers. I want to set the stage a little first before I get to the punch line.

This archery store was like any all American sportsman shop. It proudly displayed every firearm known to man, had a wide variety of archery supplies and camouflage—lots and lots of camouflage! I quickly found what I needed and headed to the checkout counter. There were about five other customers in the store along with about three or so store clerks. These fellows were clearly sportsmen. Am I painting the picture? Jack and I stuck out like a couple of sore thumbs.

We got to the counter and there, smack dab at Jack's eye level was the "Kill of the Month". It was a picture of a hunter with the buck he had shot. Jack saw the picture and suddenly burst out at the top of his lungs, "Oh my *GOSH*! Look at *THAT*! He killed a deer. How horrible! Why would someone want to kill Bambi? Why? He should be arrested! That should be illegal! Why oh why would someone do that???" The tirade went on at top volume. No amount of shushing would silence him. My feeble attempts at quieting him were not working. All eyes were on us. My attempts quickly went from, "Shush," to "It will be OK, Jack," to "Can you please be quiet?" to "We'll talk about it in the car" to "Please Jack, Please" to "Will you just *shut up*!" To the credit of all the guys in the shop, not a one of them said one word. They were very polite despite the fact a 7 year old was dragging their favorite pastime through the mud. We completed the transaction and I skulked out of the store with my outraged Bambi lover in tow.

When we got in the car, I turned to Jack. First I apologized for telling him to "Shut up" and then went on to explain why he didn't need to say out loud *everything* he was thinking *every single* time he was thinking it! We talked about how we went into their store and it was their world. When you are in someone else's territory, it is not your place to pass judgment on what they choose to do.

Teaching our kids they can't take back words they regret no matter how much they want to is an important lesson. I have used the Socrates Connection as another way to try and teach Jack this lesson.

## *The Socrates Connection*

A few years ago, I was working with an amazing woman named Karen, who was very wise and calm. I was in awe of her. My friend Amy and I were working on a presentation for an adult leadership course we were teaching, and Karen was helping us.

Karen shared something her mom always said: "Don't say anything unless it is kind, true, and necessary."

I had never heard this one before. I had heard the old adage, "If you don't have anything nice to say, don't say anything at all," but I liked this one better. It had meat on it. It really made you stop and think; which was the whole point. I later learned it might have come from the Greek Athenian philosopher, Socrates. I say *might* because there is some dispute over the actual origin of this philosophy. For me, it will always be from Karen's mom.

Here is the Socrates connection:

### SOCRATES' TRIPLE FILTER TEST

In ancient Greece, Socrates was reputed to hold knowledge in high esteem. One day an acquaintance met the great philosopher and said, "Do you know what I just heard about your friend?"

"Hold on a minute," Socrates replied. "Before you talk to me about my friend, it might be a good idea to take a moment and filter what you're going to say. That's why I call it the triple filter test. The first filter is Truth. Have you made absolutely sure that what you are about to tell me is true?"

"Well, no," the man said, "actually I just heard about it and…"

"All right," said Socrates. "So you don't really know if it's true or not. Now, let's try the second filter, the filter of Goodness. Is what you are about to tell me about my friend something good?

"Umm, no, on the contrary…"

"So," Socrates continued, "you want to tell me something bad about my friend, but you're not certain it's true. You may still pass the test though, because there's one filter left—the filter of Usefulness. Is what you want to tell me about my friend going to be useful to me?"

"No, not really."

"Well," concluded Socrates, "if what you want to tell me is neither true, nor good, nor even useful, why tell it to me at all?[39]

There is a lot of debate as to whether this was Socrates or not.

---

39   Socrates text from Inspirational Stories on-line: www.inspirationalstories.com/socrates-triple-filter-test

Frankly, it does not matter. The point is Jack and I try to use it as a test for saying things.

Is it kind? True? Necessary? If it is not all three, we don't say it.

## *Was It Safer Then?*

When I was little and our family went to a place that was not one of our usual haunts—like a stadium, a museum, or an amusement park—my mom would pick a place near the entrance and say, "If we get separated, we will meet back here." I have done this with every group of kids I have ever been in charge of.

One time, my niece and nephew spent the night with Auntie Ann and we went to the Children's Discovery Museum in our town. We agreed if we got separated we would meet at the fire truck. We were there for only five minutes when my niece, Michele, darted off to parts unknown. My nephew Mike and I looked, but we could not find her. I sent Mike running ahead to see if she had gone to the fire truck. When you tell kids, "if we get separated, we'll meet here", there is always a doubt in your mind; they will remember. I was so amazingly pleased with my niece. She did exactly what I told her to do. When I found both of them coming back from the fire truck, we all broke into tears. Honestly, I do not know who was more scared, my niece who was lost, my nephew who found her or the Auntie who was terrified she had lost her only niece! Afterwards, we hugged and had a great day.

Teach your kids how to find things, how to navigate in a public place and who to go to for help. On that day, I also took both kids by the hand and marched up to one of the museum docents.

"See what he is wearing? If you get lost, don't talk to anyone who is not wearing a uniform like this."

I do not believe it was safer when I was growing up, and the Census bears the truth. Crime in the United States has been steadily decreasing from 1980 to now—down a total of 16.8%.[40]

I am not telling you to let your kids loose on the world without teaching them how to protect themselves, but there has to be a balance. The National

---

40   U.S. Department of Justice, Federal Bureau of Investigation, *Crime in the United States,* (Washington DC: U.S. Department of Justice, September 2009)

Center for Missing and Exploited Children shows the risk of a child being kidnapped is about 1 in 1.5 million (0.00007%).[41]

Part of the process of teaching the six millionaire skills is letting our kids take action. Sometimes that action needs to be independent of us. While we need to keep safety in mind, we can't allow our fears to stop us from letting our kids grow.

## Grade Yourself

My mastermind friend Kathy offered me this wonderful parenting pearl. It is so simple, yet brilliant! Jack now makes up a mock report card for himself each quarter. I take the report card form, remove the grades and I help him fill in the grades he wants to get—complete with teacher comments! This gives Jack something to strive for all quarter long. It helps when it is time for homework too. I can gently remind him, the grade he wants to get is his goal, not mine. Thanks Kathy!

We have to operate somewhere between "helicopter parent" and a "free range parent". If we compare my mother and—dare I say it—most mothers of the past, we would have to label them "free range parents." (I can just hear my mom laughing at that one!) We have to give our kids the tools they need to help themselves in any situation, with logic, common sense and safety.

Let's all agree to stop overprotecting our kids and let them learn!

---

41   Andrea J. Sedlak, David Finkelhor, Heather Hammer, Dana J. Schultz, National Center for Missing & Exploited Children (NCMEC), and U.S. Department of Justice: *National Estimates of Missing Children: An Overview, in National Incidence Studies of Missing, Abducted, Runaway, and Thrownaway Children,* (Washington, DC: Office of Juvenile Justice and Delinquency Prevention, Office of Justice Programs, U.S. Department of Justice, October 2002)

## Conclusion

> *"I don't think I've ever worked so hard on something, but working on the Macintosh was the neatest experience of my life. Almost everyone who worked on it will say that. None of us wanted to release it at the end. It was a though we knew that once it was out of our hands it wouldn't be ours anymore."*
>
> —Steve Jobs

I don't know if I could have found a more appropriate quote to end this book. The sentiment Steve Job's felt for his work on the Mac encapsulates everything every parent feels about raising their child. You work harder at raising your kids than anything else you have ever done in your life. You agonize over even the slightest event and anguish over whether or not you have done the right thing countless times. Ultimately, when it is all said and done, you have to let them go. You have to trust they have learned all the lessons you tried to teach them. You have to let them set their own course and allow them to become the person *they* want to be. Because—like Jobs—we all know, when they grow up they are not really *ours* anymore; letting them grow and go is the hardest thing we will ever have to do in our lives.

I hope this book has fired you up and inspired you to help release the entrepreneurial genie that lives in your kids. We all have the internal capacity to "Dream It", "Believe It", "Love It", "Work It", "Own It" and "Give It". These are *learned* skills and it takes a conscious effort on our part—as parents—to help our kids learn them.

In the journey of writing this book, I have rediscovered the millionaire skills my parents taught me and have had more fun teaching those skills to Jack than I could have ever imagined.

To be honest, I am not really sure who has learned more.☺

I know for me, seeing Jack find his self-esteem again, grow into his Dyslexia, plan for college and work hard to realize his mission in life will be one of the sweetest wishes I could ever have come true. This year alone, Jack's Dad and I attended our first parent teacher conference where the kind words about Jack were not followed with, "But, …"

Unless you have a kid with a learning disability, you cannot imagine how rewarding it was for me to see my son choose to sit and read a book.

This has been an amazing few years of discovery. I can't wait for the rest of our story.

We don't know each other, but I know this about you. You cared enough about your kids to take the time to read this book. I am humbled and honored. My aspiration in writing it is that each parent who reads it will be inspired to help their kids imagine and dream the perfect life and teach them the millionaire skills they will need to live it.

At the end of the book, there were still some additional resources I wanted you to have, so I have made an extra resources page. There is a hodgepodge of information on this page.

I hope you find it helpful.

**www.howtoraiseamillionaire.com/ extraresources**

# ABOUT THE AUTHOR

Ann Morgan James is a two time award winning marketeer (Marketer of the Year and STAR Marketer of the Year), an author, speaker and Jack's mom. In the third grade, Ann's son Jack was dealt a devastating blow. He was bullied in school to the point of physical violence. His self-esteem was virtually non-existent. Ann knew she had to do something to help him.

As a marketing professional for more than 25 years Ann turned her talents for selling other people's products to her son. She began selling her son bully proof self-esteem. She decided to help him start a business and through those efforts she rebuilt his confidence and self-worth.

Ann was amazed with the results. She realized she was teaching Jack the same millionaire mindsets her parents had taught her – Outlook, Attitude, Skills and Action. To help Jack, she defined six millionaire skills she needed to teach him: "Dream It", "Believe It", "Love It", "Work It", "Own It" and "Give It". These six skills are now a philosophy she and Jack have adopted in life!

Ann has spent years volunteering and working with parents and kids. After her amazing experience with Jack she decided to share her millionaire skills with other parents and wrote her book, *How to Raise a Millionaire.*

She is also one of the featured entrepreneurs in *Entrepreneur success stories: how common people achieve uncommon results, volume two* edited by Loral Langemeier and John C. Robinson.

Aside from the credentials and awards Ann has earned, she is first and foremost, Jack's Mom. Other parents will surely identify with her. With her challenges in her life; challenges she has faced down head-on and overcome, Ann has a story of hope and inspiration to tell.

Ann has one passion which drives her to overcome any bump in the road life throws her way; she is determined to teach her son Jack how to live the life of his dreams.

Ann is a native California girl who lives in San Jose with her son Jack, their three dogs, one parrot and every single Star Wars: The Clone Wars action figure known to man!☺

*Meet Our Family*

# RESOURCES

- **Howtoraiseamillionaire.com**

  To help you teach your kids our six millionaire skills, we have worked hard to develop a suite of products to support you in your mission to "Dream It", "Believe It", "Love It", "Work It", "Own It" and "Give It".

  We have divided our products into three categories: Information, Inspiration and Implementation. Here are just a few of the products you'll find at howtoraiseamillionaire.com

- **Fast Start Action Guide:** *Take your kid from chores to Entrepreneur in 5 days*

  Our Fast Start Action Guide is a step-by-step interactive workbook you can use to get your kid's business up and running in five days. It is complete with collaboration activities for you and your kids to play, sample forms, flyers, and brochures you can use to get up and running without having to reinvent the wheel. If you are looking for the playbook on how to help your kid start their own business, our easy and quick Fast Start Action Guide is for you.

- **Dream It Millionaire Skill Action Guide**

  Teaching a child to dream might seem like a simple thing to do. All kids have a great imagination, right? My guide helps you enable them to turn their imagination inward so they can see themselves and their potential. The guide provides you with a step-by-step way to help your kids uncover their dreams, big and small!

- **Believe It Millionaire Skill Action Guide**

  Confidence and self-esteem are two of the hardest things to teach our kids. It is not easy in our overly competitive world. This action guide gives you some real life practical things to do to help build your kids confidence. Helping them believe in themselves is probably one of the most important skills you can teach your children. Resilience is learned at home! Start today!

- **Love It Millionaire Skill Action Guide**
Passion for the things you love, the ones you love and the ideals you hold is a driving force that can take a person from ordinary to extraordinary! This action guide helps you stoke the fires that burn inside your child. They help you navigate through the pitfalls we easily fall into. Fueling and directing their passion is hard work! Our action guide is designed to give you ideas to make it easier.

- **Work It Millionaire Skill Action Guide**
How do you teach your kids to give 110% on every job? What can we—as parents—do to help them see the value in doing a job right the first time? This guide gives you ideas and suggestions on how to turn up the dial on your kid's responsibility meter.

- **Own It Millionaire Skill Action Guide**
Being able to say, "I did it, it was my decision," is hard for an adult. How do we teach it to our kids? This guide shows you ways to take your kid from a finger pointer to a stand up kid. It gives you ideas and a course of action you can take to help your child take responsibility for their actions.

- **Give It Millionaire Skill Action Guide**
The rewards of giving can change your life. Teaching your child to be compassionate, caring and giving to those around them might be the greatest millionaire skill. It certainly is the most rewarding. Teaching our kids to serve others helps them become a better sibling, son or daughter, student and member of the world stage. It is the pie in the sky stuff that nirvana is make of and I am not ashamed to say I wrote an action guide to help anyone raise a better human being!

- **How to Raise a Millionaire Vision Book (for teens)**
Being a teenager in today's world is challenging, but this tool can help you in many ways. Visionbooking shows you how to deliberately create a visual image of the life and future you desire. The process is empowering, insightful, fun...and it works for everyone and every type of goal or aspiration! You will learn more about who you are right now, who you really want to become and how to get there.

- **How to Raise a Millionaire Vision Book (for adults)**
  Nothing is more powerful than doing things with your child. Visionbooking shows you how to create the life of your dreams. Model visionbooking for your kids and show them you believe in the lessons you are teaching. When you do a vision book with your kids, you show them just how much you believe in dreaming! You'll have a lot of fun too.☺ I promise!

- **Popsicle Pros Sticks**
  If you loved the Parenting Pearl about Popsicle Pros you'll love having these powerful sticks of your own. You can order our Popsicle Pros Sticks to keep in your car, kitchen or wherever you think they will come in handy. Start each morning off with a positive affirmation that will last all day. Our sticks are available in various quantities. Be sure to order enough for yourself! ☺

- **Confidence Coins**
  Compliments and positive feedback build your child's confidence. Negative remarks and feedback can be hard to take and even harder to overcome. The trick is to compliment more than you criticize. Confidence Coins are a simple tool you can use to gently remind yourself to compliment first before you criticize. The rule of thumb is 10 compliments to 1 criticism. Use our Confidence Coins to help build self-esteem and confidence. We are all human and it is easy to forget in the heat of the battle. When I have my coins in my pocket it reminds me to compliment first.

*See our*
*Resources*

# *Join our*
# HOW TO RAISE A MILLIONAIRE
## *Community!*

Let's be honest, I don't know it all and neither do you! But together, we sure can hedge our bets and we certainly know a lot more when we work as a community of parents and caregivers.

We are building an amazing group of like-minded parents who want to help their kids live the life of their dreams.

We are pulling together information from a number of sources, not just me and certainly not just one point of view. As a member of this community you have the exclusive opportunity to access all our tools. We'll tackle a variety of topics to help you coach your kids. We are creating a forum where you can get information as well as give it.

*Join our*
*Community*

Below is a *unique number* you can use to access the community. This number will give you *3 months free access*. This is our gift to you. We are confident you will find the information on the site valuable.

Here are just a few of our member benefits:

- You'll receive our Members Only Newsletter once a month telling you what is new on the site!
- You'll get exclusive invitations and discounts to events and seminars.
- *Free Resources.* We'll provide you with articles, papers, e-books and more. These tools will be acquired monthly on your behalf from our many partners.
- As a member of our community, you'll also receive a 10% discount on any future product purchases made from our website.

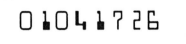

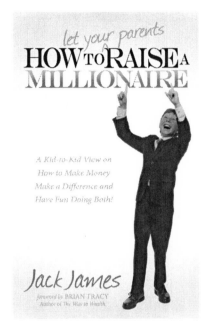

*let your parents*

# HOW TO RAISE A MILLIONAIRE

*A Kid-to-Kid View on How to Make Money Make a Difference and Have Fun Doing Both!*

Jack James

*foreword by BRIAN TRACY*
*Author of The Way to Wealth*

## JACK'S BOOK!

Don't forget to pick up a copy of Jack's book for your kids. His book is the inspiring story of how he started his business, what he has learned and why every kid should start their own business and become an entrepreneur.

His book is written from one kid to another.

In addition, he wrote a chapter about what it was like to be bullied and a chapter about having a learning disability. In these chapters, he tells how he built in himself *Bully-Proof Self-Esteem*. His words of encouragement to other kids are stirring. He is honest and straight-forward. Regardless of whether your children are struggling or not, they will no doubt gain strength from the honest and heartfelt words of a fellow kid.

*Buy Jack's Book*

**How to raise a millionaire : Six millionaire**
649.6 MOR                                    00060434

| DATE DUE | | | |
|---|---|---|---|
|  |  |  |  |
|  |  |  |  |
|  |  |  |  |
|  |  |  |  |
|  |  |  |  |
|  |  |  |  |
|  |  |  |  |
|  |  |  |  |
|  |  |  |  |
|  |  |  |  |
|  |  |  |  |
|  |  |  |  |

NC

CPSIA information can be obtained at www.ICGtesting.com
Printed in the USA
LVOW081308301012

305069LV00002B/2/P

9 781614 482468